THE

MISSION OF THE SPIRIT;

OR,

THE OFFICE AND WORK OF THE COMFORTER IN HUMAN REDEMPTION.

BY REV. L. R. DUNN.

"Ὁ δὲ παράκλητος, τὸ πνεῦμα τὸ ἅγιον."—JOHN xiv, 26.

SECOND EDITION.

NEW YORK:
CARLTON & LANAHAN
SAN FRANCISCO: E. THOMAS.
CINCINNATI: HITCHCOCK & WALDEN.
1872.

PREFACE.

THIS is the dispensation of the Spirit. We are living in the very midst of its culminating glories. The rushing fires of another Pentecost are coming upon the Church now as they have not during the centuries preceding the one in which we live. All eyes are lifted expectant to the everlasting hills, where intercedes a glorified and exalted Christ. Or ever his triumphal chariot had wheeled upward to the gates of pearl, he left his promise and his pledge to the Church of the wonderful gift of the Comforter. That promise and that pledge have only been fulfilled in part—in individual instances and in certain localities. The Church, overrun with worldliness and beclouded by unbelief, has been comparatively powerless for the want of the full baptism of the Comforter. And the world, this poor, lost, fallen world, still remains unransomed from its sins and their consequences. The great work of preparation for its complete redemption seems, however, well-nigh finished. The mountains have been leveled, and the valleys upreared; the crooked places have been straightened, and the rough places smoothened, and the time for "all flesh to see the salvation of our God" is at hand.

What is now wanted is a universal pentecost, not only that all the babbling millions of earth may hear of "the wonderful works of God" in their "own tongue wherein they were born," but that they may be "pricked to the heart" by the arrows of the convincing Spirit, and be saved by his power.

It is a somewhat remarkable fact that, with all the teachings of the Divine Head in reference to the Comforter, with all the luminous promises of his gifts and grace, so little, comparatively, has been written concerning him. The world is full of books about Christ, and the number of them is constantly increasing; but we can almost count on our finger ends the books written specifically about the Holy Ghost. And yet his sovereign agency in the completion and consummation of redemption's work is constantly acknowledged in the word of God. Why this is so, that so little has been written, we can scarcely tell; and yet, because it is so, there is much of ignorance, doubt, and unbelief in the Church as to his work and his power. Many huge volumes of theology devote only a few pages to the consideration of his Godhead, his offices, and his work. There is now and then a sermon preached upon these all-important themes; but too seldom are they introduced into the sacred desk.

The author of this book has long felt that a treatise bearing directly upon these questions is a *desideratum* in the literature of the Christian Church. In conversation with several leading divines in his own and other denominations, he has found that they entertained the same views and feelings, and he has been encouraged by their advice to proceed with the preparation of this volume. How successful he may have been in the performance of his work the reader will judge. Due acknowledgment has been made of the authors from whose works quotations have been made, in foot-notes, and therefore no mention of their names is needed here.

The author fully believes that the coming and the crowning conflict of the Church will be about the truths dwelt upon in this volume.

Indeed, there is, even now, "skirmishing all along the line." The great aim of modern infidelity is to ignore all spiritual agencies ; to banish God from the world ; to deny all miraculous agency and all moral regeneration ; to proclaim a cold, dull, dead materialism ; and to bind the universe in the chains of fixed, irreversible and inviolable law. If the writer has made it to appear that there is not only a supernatural and superhuman, but a Divine Agency, working out great spiritual results, and effecting great moral regenerations—an agent who, because he is God, is capable of bringing about the complete transformation and revivification of a fallen and dead humanity, and who is able and willing and ready to do this work now—he will be glad that he has contributed something that will serve to call attention to the ever-blessed Comforter.

Bespeaking the indulgence of the critical reader, and beseeching the earnest, prayerful reading of this book by all classes of the ministry and laity of the evangelical Churches, the author sends forth this volume with many prayers that all may find a "blessing in it."

L. R. D.

ST. PAUL'S PARSONAGE, *Elizabeth, N. J.*

CONTENTS.

VENI SANCTE SPIRITUS.*

I.

Veni, Sancte Spiritus,
Et emitte cœlitus,
  Lucis tuæ radium.
Veni, pater pauperum,
Veni, dator munerum,
  Veni lumen cordium.

II.

Consolator optime,
Dulcis hospes animæ,
  Dulce refrigerium.
In labore requies,
In æstu temperies,
  In fletu solatium.

III.

O lux beatissima !
Reple cordis intima
  Tuorum fidelium.
Sine tuo numine,
Nihil est in homine,
  Nihil est innoxium.

* Written at the beginning of the eleventh century.

The following translation of this inimitable hymn is from the chaste and elegant pen of Dr. Abraham Coles of Newark, N. J.

I.

Come, O Holy Spirit, come,
And from Thy celestial home
  Of Thy light a ray impart!
Come Thou, Father of the poor!
Come Thou, giver of heaven's store!
  Come Thou, light of every heart!

II.

Promised Comforter, and best,
Of the soul the dearest Guest,
  Sweet Refreshment here below,
Rest, in labor, to the feet,
Coolness in the scorching heat,
  Solace in the time of woe.

III.

O most blessed Light! the heart's
Innermost, most hidden parts
  Of Thy faithful people, fill!
Not without Thy favor can
Any thing be good in man,
  Any thing that is not ill.

IV.

Lava quod est sordidum,
Riga quod est aridum
  Sana quod est saucium !
Flecte quod est rigidum,
Fove quod est frigidum
  Rege quod est devium !

V.

Da tuis fidelibus,
In te confidentibus,
  Sanctum septenarium : *
Da virtutis meritum,
Da salutis exitium,
  Da perenne gaudium !

ROBERTUS REX FRANCIÆ.

* The seven gifts of the Spirit.

IV.

What is sordid make Thou clean ;
What is dry make moist and green;
  What is wounded heal for aye.
Bend what's rigid to Thy will;
Warm Thou whatsoe'er is chill;
  Guide what's devious and astray.

V.

To thy faithful given be—
Those confiding still in Thee—
  Graciously the holy seven ;
Give Thou virtue's recompense,
Give a safe departure hence,
  Give th' eternal joy of heaven.

THE

MISSION OF THE SPIRIT.

CHAPTER I.

PERSONALITY AND GODHEAD OF THE COMFORTER.

"I BELIEVE in the Holy Ghost." So universal Christendom has given utterance to its *credo* during the roll of the centuries. But while this utterance has been uniform and universal, the interpretations given to it have widely differed. The Greek Church, while holding to his essential Godhead, teaches that he "proceeds only from the Father." The Romish, as well as the Evangelical Protestant Church, holds to the procession "from the Father and the Son." The Unitarian or Socinian Church, however differing in its views as to the character of Christ, denies the personality and Godhead of the Holy Ghost, and looks upon him as merely an attribute, an emanation, or an influence. For ages past fierce controversies have been waged by those occupying these different stand-points. The history of these controversies is of deep interest to the Christian scholar ; but it is no part of the design of this volume to enter upon this field.

Nor is this struggle yet ended. It is more than probable that as Atheism has denied the existence of God, and as Arianism has denied the divinity of Christ, so the enemies of God and of his truth will assail the divinity and personality of the Holy Ghost. This, indeed, may be the last great struggle which the "Truth of God" may have to endure before the glories of millennial day shall burst upon this world. The struggle with the Atheist is over. The struggle with the Rationalist, Pantheist, Spiritualist, and Scientist must soon close ; but the struggle with the "blasphemers against the Holy Ghost" is coming on. I would do my part toward preparing the Church for this final conflict. In so doing, I shall endeavor to state, illustrate, and enforce the teachings of the word of the Lord concerning the character and perfections of the Paraclete, and his offices and relations in the economy of human redemption.

I shall now undertake to prove that the *Holy Ghost is a Person distinct from the Father and the Son, and not merely an Attribute or an Emanation from either.* The evidence adduced to sustain this position is from the word of God. In the very nature of the case there is, there can be, no other. No man can read that word with any degree of care without noticing that there is a Being constantly referred to as acting with the Father, or with the Son, or with both; and that that Being is called by the names, bears the titles, possesses the attributes, and performs the acts of God. Masculine pronouns and relatives in the Greek of the New Testament are used with the neuter noun πνευμα—spirit; thus showing that the writers of its books intended to teach his personality. "I will pray the Father, and he shall give you another Comforter, that he may abide with you forever; even the Spirit of truth; whom the world cannot receive, because it seeth him not, neither knoweth him: but ye know him; for he dwelleth with you, and shall be in you." John xiv, 16, 17. "But the Comforter, which is the Holy Ghost, whom the Father will send in my name, he shall teach you all things." John xiv, 26. "But when the Comforter is come, whom I will send unto you from the Father, even the Spirit of truth, which proceedeth from the Father, he shall testify of me." John xv, 26. "And when he is come, he will reprove the world of sin." John xvi, 8. "When he, the Spirit of truth, is come, he will guide you into all truth: for he shall not speak of himself; but whatsoever he shall hear, that shall he speak: and he will show you things to come. He shall glorify me: for he shall receive of mine." John xvi, 13, 14. Now any interpretation which makes the Holy Spirit an Attribute or an Emanation renders these, and many other portions of the word of God, utterly unmeaning.

It is well known that at the first Arius regarded the Holy Ghost as a creature, created by Christ; but afterward his personality was denied by the Arians; and the view since held by them is that he is the exerted energy, or power, of God. Let us regard this view in the light of other portions of the word of God.

"God anointed Jesus of Nazareth with the Holy Ghost and with power." Acts x, 38. The Arian interpretation would make it read, "God anointed Jesus with the holy power of God, and with power." Again, "Now the God of hope fill you with all joy and peace in believing, that ye may abound in hope, through the power of the Holy Ghost." Rom. xv, 13. That is, according to the Arian view, by the power of the holy power of God. "Through mighty signs and wonders, by the power of the Spirit of God." Rom. xv, 19. That is, mighty signs and wonders by the power of the power of God. "In demonstration of the Spirit and of power." 1 Cor. ii, 4. That is, demonstration of the power and of power. These portions of Scripture are sufficient to prove his personality, and to show the senselessness of the Arian interpretation. But the Paraclete is not only a person; he is also a *divine person.* To prove this, I shall proceed to show that the *Names*, the *Attributes*, and the *Acts* of God are ascribed to him.

1. And first the *Names*. The apostle Peter said to Ananias, "Why hath Satan filled thine heart to lie to the Holy Ghost?... Thou hast not lied unto men, but unto God." Acts v, 3, 4. Here we see that the Holy Ghost is called God. "Now the Lord is that Spirit." 2 Cor. iii, 17. "For who hath known the mind of the Lord, that he may instruct him?" 1 Cor. ii, 16. "For who hath known the mind of the Lord? or who hath been his coun-

selor?" Rom. xi, 34. Both these passages are evidently quotations from Isaiah: "Who hath directed the Spirit of the Lord, or being his Counselor hath taught him?" Isa. xl, 13. "And the Lord direct your hearts into the love of God, and into the patient waiting for Christ." 2 Thess. iii, 5. Now this person, thus prayerfully addressed, is called the Lord, is regarded as able to direct the hearts of the Thessalonians, and to inspire them with patience; and prayer is offered to him by an inspired apostle. Yet he is evidently neither God the Father nor God the Son. Hence we see that the highest names, "God" and "the Lord," are given to the Holy Ghost.

2. With equal clearness the *Attributes of God* are ascribed to him.

Eternity.—"Christ, who through the eternal Spirit offered himself without spot to God." Heb. ix, 14.

Omnipotence.—This is so frequently ascribed to him as to seem to afford some show of reason for the Arian view that he is the power of God.

Omniscience.—"The Spirit searcheth all things, yea, the deep things of God." "The things of God knoweth no man, but the Spirit of God." 1 Cor. ii, 10, 11.

Omnipresence.—"Whither shall I go from thy Spirit? or whither shall I flee from thy presence?" Psa. cxxxix, 7. "What! know ye not that your body is the temple of the Holy Ghost which is in you?" 1 Cor. vi, 19. But this is said of all believers. Now, then, if the body of each Christian is the temple of the Holy Ghost, then he must be present with, and abide in, a multitude at the same time, and in widely different localities; and to do this he must be omnipresent.

Holiness.—"The Holy Ghost." "Holy Spirit." "Spirit of Holiness." And in the New Testament he bears this emphatic name no less than ninety-three times.*

Truth.—"When he, the Spirit of truth, is come." John xvi, 13.

Goodness.—"Thy good Spirit," Neh. ix, 20. "Thy Spirit is good." Psa. cxliii, 10.

Glory.—"The spirit of glory and of God." 1 Pet. iv, 14.

3. The *Acts of God* are ascribed to him.

Creation.—"The Spirit of God moved upon the face of the waters." Gen. i, 2. "By his Spirit he hath garnished the heavens." Job xxvi, 13.

* Spirit of Life, p. 53.

"The Spirit of God hath made me." Job xxxiii, 4.

The *power of working miracles*, which the inspired writers explicitly declare is of God, is said to belong to him.

Inspiration.—Paul, writing to the Hebrews, says, "God spake unto the fathers by the prophets." Heb. i, 1. And Peter says, "Holy men of God spake as they were moved by the Holy Ghost." 2 Pet. i, 21. Also, that it was "the Spirit of Christ which was in them" which "testified beforehand the sufferings of Christ, and the glory that should follow." 1 Pet. i, 11.

Quickening.—"It is the Spirit that quickeneth." John vi, 63. "Quickened by the Spirit." 1 Pet. iii, 18. "Shall also quicken your mortal bodies by his Spirit that dwelleth in you." Rom. viii, 11.

4. The Holy Ghost is acknowledged in his personality and Godhead in the formula of Christian Baptism, and in the solemn and impressive form of benediction—"Baptizing them in the name of the Father, and of the Son, and of the Holy Ghost." Matt. xxviii, 19. "The grace of the Lord Jesus Christ, and the love of God, and the communion of the Holy Ghost." 2 Cor. xiii, 14. Now, if the Arian interpretation

be correct, then these formulas are in the name of one God, one creature, and one attribute or emanation.

5. In many parts of Scripture the Holy Ghost is associated with the Father and the Son in *acts, titles, authority*, and *worship*, and is spoken of, or addressed, as of *equal power, glory*, and *authority*. For instance, in the Old Testament Scriptures we read as follows: "And now the Lord God, and his Spirit, hath sent me." Isa. xlviii, 16. "I am with you, saith the Lord of Hosts: according to the word that I covenanted with you when ye came out of Egypt, so my Spirit remaineth among you: fear ye not. And I will shake all nations, and the desire of all nations shall come." Hag. ii, 4, 7. Here is God the Father speaking of his Spirit and promising the advent of his Son. "The Lord of Hosts," whom Isaiah declared spoke to him, the apostle says was the Holy Ghost: "I heard the voice of the Lord, saying, Whom shall I send?" etc. Isa. vi, 8–10. And, "Well spake the Holy Ghost by Esaias the prophet unto our fathers." Acts xxviii, 25. It may be well here to add that the Apostle John says that in this sublime vision and call of the prophet he saw the

glory of Christ. "These things said Esaias, when he saw his glory"—the glory of Christ—"and spake of him." John xii, 41. It was in view of the presence of the three persons in the Godhead in this vision, doubtless, that the six-winged seraphim cried, "Holy, holy, holy, is the Lord of hosts!" Isa. vi, 3. To come to the New Testament Scriptures: here we find at the baptism of Christ the presence of the Father and of his Holy Spirit. After his baptism, "The heavens were opened unto him, and he saw the Spirit of God descending like a dove, and lighting upon him. And lo a voice from heaven, saying, This is my beloved Son, in whom I am well pleased." Matt. iii, 16, 17. Here is the Father speaking from heaven, acknowledging the one just baptized by John as his beloved Son; and here is, also, the Spirit, distinct from both, and yet in harmony and union with both, anointing the Son of God and the Son of man for his work.

In the great work of saving the sinner, and of adopting him into the divine family, the Spirit is said to be associated with the Father and the Son in a number of places. Take only the following: "Because ye are sons, God hath sent forth the Spirit of his Son into your hearts, crying, Abba, Father." Gal. iv, 6. "After that the kindness and love of God our Saviour toward man appeared, . . . according to his mercy he saved us, by the washing of regeneration, and renewing of the Holy Ghost; which he shed on us abundantly through Jesus Christ our Saviour." Titus iii, 4–6. These proofs might be greatly multiplied. They are, in fact, so abundant that to quote all legitimately bearing upon these several points would occupy a large part of the present volume. Here are enough to convince any honest mind of the distinct personality and essential Godhead of the Holy Ghost.

Let us, therefore, bow before the throne, and devoutly say, "Glory be to the Father, and to the Son, and to the Holy Ghost! As it was in the beginning, is now, and ever shall be, world without end! Amen."

CHAPTER II.

THE PROMISE OF THE COMFORTER.

EIGHT hundred years before the advent of Christ, the Prophet Joel heralded the coming of the Comforter in the following language: "And it shall come to pass afterward that I will pour out my Spirit upon all flesh; and your sons and your daughters shall prophesy, your old men shall dream dreams, your young men shall see visions: and also upon the servants and upon the handmaids in those days will I pour out my Spirit." Joel ii, 28, 29. All down those centuries this promise was uttered, until it had its first grand and signal fulfillment upon the day of Pentecost. So clearly and fully indeed was it fulfilled that the Apostle Peter unhesitatingly declared, "*This is* that which was spoken by the Prophet Joel." Acts ii, 16. John the Baptist, recognizing the great mission and work of the Divine Redeemer, proclaimed of him, "He shall baptize you with the Holy Ghost, and with fire." Matt. iii, 11.

At length he came, "The Desire of all Nations," and for the space of three years his wonderful ministry was exercised among men. Not, however, until toward its close did he announce the coming of the mighty Comforter. It was then, when the disciples were sad and sorrowing at the announcement of his departure from them, when they felt that they were going to be orphaned, and the future looked dark and dreary to them, that he promised, upon the event of his departure, to send to them the Comforter, the richest gift of heaven. "If I depart, I will send him unto you." John xvi, 7. The promises now began to multiply, and the sweet and gracious assurances of an ever-abiding Comforter were unstintedly given to them. "I will pray the Father, and he shall give you another Comforter, that he may abide with you forever; even the Spirit of truth; whom the world cannot receive, because it seeth him not, neither knoweth him: but ye know him; for he dwelleth with you, and shall be in you." John xiv, 16, 17. "But the Comforter, which is the Holy Ghost, whom the Father will send in my name." John xiv, 26. "But when the Comforter is come, whom I will send unto you from the Father, even the Spirit of truth, which proceedeth from the Father, he shall testify of me." John xv, 26. "And when he [the Comforter] is come, he will reprove the world," etc. John xvi, 8–11. "Howbeit, when he, the Spirit of truth, is come, he will guide you into all truth," etc. John xvi, 13–14. After his resurrection the Son of God repeated his promise, and proclaimed the near advent of the Comforter. "But ye shall receive power, after that the Holy Ghost is come upon you: and ye shall be witnesses unto me." Acts i, 8. Again, "Behold, I send the promise of my Father upon you: but tarry ye in the city of Jerusalem, until ye be endued with power from on high." Luke xxiv, 49. "Ye shall be baptized with the Holy Ghost not many days hence." Acts i, 5. It was, doubtless, for the fulfillment of this promise that they tarried in the upper room at Jerusalem, and held their ten days' prayer-meeting. Let us here note,

1. *These promises are clear and explicit.* "I *will* send him unto you." "The Father *will* send him in my name." "If ye then, being evil, know how to give good gifts unto your children; how much more shall your heavenly Father

give the Holy Spirit to them that ask him?" Luke xi, 13. There was no room for doubt in the minds of the early disciples; nor after Christ's resurrection did they seem to have any doubt or misgiving as to the bestowment of this gift. What thoughts may have entered into their minds as they waited day after day and prayed for, and expected, the gift so freely promised, we know not. We can readily conceive how dark shadows of doubt might have flitted across their minds as the promise was delayed. How they might have said to one another, "Have we misunderstood the promise?" "Are we asking aright for this gift?" "Why, then, is it delayed?" But if these thoughts passed through their minds they were quickly dispelled, and faith triumphed. If such questionings had risen in their minds the answer would doubtless have been ready and prompt. "We cannot misunderstand that promise. He certainly said that if he should go away he would send us the Comforter; and he has gone away. We saw him in his great ascent; we beheld him go up into heaven. He is certainly there. And then, too, we are asking for this gift in his name, as he told us to ask. We will pray on. The promise must be fulfilled."

It may be also that they tried to imagine to themselves how the Comforter would come. Perhaps some of them who knew of the scenes which had occurred at the baptism of their Lord thought he would come in a bodily shape, like a dove brooding over them, and thus visibly abide among them. Others, mayhap, rose in the fullness of their faith to the conception that this was to be an inward gift, unaccompanied by external signs ; a gift unseen by mortal eye, but to be consciously felt in the very depths of their spiritual being. But, whatever were their thoughts, they still prayed on in anxious, yet undoubting expectation of the coming of the promised Comforter.

O what a model is this for the Church in all the ages ! We, too, have the promise, not uttered from memory, but right before our eyes in the blessed book. We can put our finger upon it and look up. There is no darkness or obscurity about it. It is clear as the light of heaven. It is sustained by the immutability and omnipotence of the Son of God. There is really no room for doubt or fear as to its truth or as to its actual fulfillment. Then, too, we have an advantage which they did not possess. The promise to us is a *tried* promise. But they had no one to say to them, "I know what this gift is; I have received it; pray on, you will certainly receive it." But we have the accumulated testimony of centuries, and of countless thousands of believers who have received this gift and felt the power of the Holy Ghost in every avenue of their being. The saints of eighteen centuries bear witness to this truth.

2. *This promise is universal.* This was not merely a gift for the apostles and their contemporaries, but for every clime and every age. The prophecy of Joel had clearly settled this point: "I will pour out my Spirit *upon all flesh.*" And the Apostle Peter, under the plenary inspiration of the Comforter, after quoting this promise, made of it the most unlimited application. "The promise is to you," —all that were there gathered together—"Jews, devout men, from every nation under heaven;" and, more than this, "it is to your children"—your descendants in all the future ages; and, more than this, "it is to all who are afar off"—to the Gentile world, so spoken of by the apos-

tle in his letter to the Ephesians, (ii, 17;) and more than this, it is "even to as many as the Lord our God shall call." Acts ii, 39. No language could more clearly point out the universality of the promise than this. It just as certainly proclaims the promise to every person, in every age, and clime, as if an angel from heaven had personally addressed him, and said, "The promise of the Holy Ghost is to you;" or as if his name were written in pencilings of light on the tablet of the sky, and under it the assurance, "The promise of the Holy Ghost is to you." O then, child of God, grasp the promise! It is yours in all its freeness, richness, and fullness; and it is yours *now*. It is yours every day, hour, and moment of your history, and sooner shall the blue arch above you shrivel into atoms, and the mighty earth upon which you stand melt away, than this promise shall fail.

3. *The Comforter is promised as an abiding gift.* How often I have thought of the time when the promise of the Comforter first fell upon the saddened hearts of the disciples. They might have asked, "Lord, how long will *he* abide with us? Thou hast been with us only a little while,

and now *thou* art going away. How long will the other Comforter of whom thou hast spoken abide with us?" And O, how must their hearts have been cheered by the announcement, "*He shall abide with you forever.*" Yes; *forever!* There was to be no intermission of his presence, of his gifts, of his grace or power, in the hearts of true believers. No matter where they might be, or what might be their circumstances or conditions, believing, this gift would be theirs, and, according to the promise, so has it been, and so will it be until the end of time. This was gloriously realized in the first three centuries of the history of the Church, and it has been realized in every century since. It is his presence and power which have kept the Church alive amid the persecutions of Pagan and of Papal Rome. His presence abode with the martyred saints while endungeoned, or exiled, or driven into the dens and caves of the mountains, or hunted like beasts of prey, or fighting with beasts at Ephesus and Rome, or gored by wild bulls, or torn to pieces by hungry lions and tigers, or burned at the stake, or decapitated on the block; every-where, at all times, all along the ages, the Holy Ghost has abode in the Church. He has never left this redeemed world, and he never will until the "last trump shall sound." It is his presence which has kept alive and brightly burning the flames of divine truth and love in the hearts of the Waldenses amid the everlasting snows and ice of the Alps. This inspired and empowered Wiclif, Huss and Jerome, Luther, Melanchthon, Zwingle, Farel, La Fevre, Calvin, Knox, and their followers ; and this, during the last century and a quarter, girded the Wesleys, Whitefield, their co-laborers and successors, so that they were able to shake the whole civilized world, and to be the instruments in commencing a revival, the consummaion of which will be seen only amid the bursting glories of the millennium.

4. *The first grand fulfillment of the promise.* It was on the tenth day after they had seen their Lord and Master "go into heaven"—"when the day of Pentecost had fully come"—that they were again found assembled together in the upper room. It was early in the morning, how early we do not know. "But it must have been very early : for after they had prayed and received the baptism, and all Jerusalem was filled with the noise of what had occurred, Peter reminded the multitude that it was only the

'third hour of the day, or nine o'clock in the morning." * "They were all now with one accord in one place." Although the promise had been long delayed, still their faith did not waver; their courage was undaunted. It is not improbable that they had been looking forward to the day of Pentecost as the time when this gift of power was to be bestowed upon them. They may have said one to another, "Was not Pentecost the time when the Lord descended upon Mount Sinai, amid 'thunderings and lightnings, the voice of a trumpet and the sound of words,' and formally inaugurated the dispensation of the law? And may not this anniversary of that grand event be the chosen and ordained period when the Holy Ghost will come down upon Mount Zion, and inaugurate the new dispensation?" However this may be, there they were, all of the disciples, one hundred and twenty in number, not one absent. There was no dissentient voice, no doubting Thomas, no trembling, affrighted Peter, no weeping Mary, Heart beat responsive to heart; faith was linked to faith: prayer was mingled with prayer; and all eyes were lifted up to the hills whence they expected

* Tongue of Fire, p. 33.

"the Comforter" would come, when "suddenly there came a sound as of a rushing mighty wind." It was not wind, but a sound like the rushing of the wind. It did not come in at the window, nor through the door, but it came right "down from heaven." The sound was not natural; it was preternatural. When God appeared of old to Elijah, there was not only a fire and an earthquake, but a tempest which rent the rocks asunder, and made the whole mountain tremble under its power. Now again the sound of the "rushing mighty wind" heralds the approach of the Lord—the Holy Ghost. They understood the sign. Awed, subdued, overpowered, they fell upon their knees or upon their faces, as Elijah had done, and then the mighty baptism came—came thrilling and throbbing through every part of their being—hallowing and inspiring them with his presence and grace, emboldening them for their great work, filling them with unutterable peace and joy, and causing their tongues to speak the praises of the Lord.

And now, with eyes kindled with celestial fire, with faces all aglow with the inward rapture of their souls, and their whole being pulsating with the new, divine life, they ventured to look up, and "John sees Peter's head crowned with fire, Peter sees James crowned with fire, James sees Nathanael crowned with fire, Nathanael sees Mary crowned with fire, and round and round the fire sits 'on each of them.'" *

Thus, while they were anointed with the Holy Ghost to be the *priests* of the new dispensation, they were also crowned with coronals of fire as the kings of the Lord our God. It was, indeed, the befitting inauguration of a kingdom, all of whose subjects were to be "kings and priests." It is well for us to pause a moment at this point and notice that, vast and important as was the work which was given them to do—although the world was perishing all around them—notwithstanding during those ten days, while they were waiting and praying, thousands of immortal beings went down into their graves, and were ushered into eternal realities—yet, they were not allowed to open their lips to proclaim the Gospel until they had been "endued with power from on high." It would, in fact, have been useless for them to attempt this work without this baptism. They would

* Tongue of Fire, p. 34.

not only have lacked the grand, essential qualification for it, but their ministry would have proved a failure without it. *The time was not lost while they tarried.* Nor is that time lost by the minister or the Church which is spent in pleading for the Holy Ghost. O how often are both impatient to engage in labor for the salvation of souls, for the overthrow of Satan's kingdom, and, commencing without proper qualifications, they are routed, discomfited, mortified and discouraged! It will not do now, any more than in the olden time, for Israel to attack his enemies unless the ark of God is with him; but if the ark is with him, and he is fitted to bear it, there will be "the shout of a king in the camp." O ye ministers of Jesus, go not forth to this work unless the baptism is upon you! O ye followers of Christ, see well to it that ye are anointed with this power! If the whole Church, in its ministry and membership, were thus, as the disciples were, waiting before God day and night for this baptism, how soon would it arise and shine! how soon would it be lifted up to the platform of a blood-purchased holiness, and thence would radiate the world with its light, and shake it to its very center with its power! The immediate results of that early pentecostal morning baptism have astonished the world for nearly two thousand years, while the outgoing influences from it have traveled down all the centuries, and are felt now in every part of the wide world. I need not repeat the immediate results of that baptism. They are well known to all. Timid disciples—one of whom, and he the chief, had denied his Lord, and the rest had fled in terror; who after his crucifixion had abandoned all hope, who had even doubted his resurrection when proclaimed to them by the women—now came forth boldly and preached Jesus and the resurrection, braving the Jewish Sanhedrim and the whole power of the Roman empire; and their first day's preaching harvested three thousand souls.

It was not many days after this, when persecution began to rage against them, when the council, swayed by mingled emotions of rage and alarm, threatened them with imprisonment and death if they persisted in preaching Jesus, that another baptism of the Spirit came upon them. The prayer which they offered upon that occasion is remarkable, not for its length, nor its learnedness, but for its simplicity and its courageous faith. And when that prayer was ended, the very place where they assembled "was shaken, and they were all filled with the Holy Ghost." We are not to regard these as the only baptisms which they received. They were only grand specimens of the daily experience of the Church. And what was the daily experience of the Church then may be the daily experience of the Church now. Are we praying for it? Are we believing and holding fast to the promise? Are we, even now, looking up to the heavens and expecting his descent upon us? Then he will come not placeing coronals of fire upon our brows, not preceded by the rushing mighty wind, not shaking the place where we are praying, mayhap, but just as really, just as fully, and just as gloriously anointing us with his graces and his power.

"Come, Holy Ghost, for thee we call;
Spirit of burning, *come!*"

CHAPTER III.

THE GIFT OF THE COMFORTER THE EVIDENCE OF CHRIST'S ASCENSION AND MEDIATION.

IN the very midst of his labors and toils the Son of God declared, "My Father worketh hitherto, and I work." John v, 17. But his work upon the earth was completed when he had offered himself a sacrifice for sin, and had risen from the dead, and had given to his Church her grand commission; then, in the sight of them all, he was "taken up into heaven." He had frequently declared unto them that he "must go away; that it was expedient for them that he should go away." John xvi, 7. But he had also promised, If I go away I will send you another Comforter, that he may abide with you forever. (John xiv, 16; xvi, 7.) He had also said unto them, when sorrow was filling their hearts, "If I go not away, the Comforter will not come unto you; but if I depart, *I will send him unto you.*" John xvi, 7. The bestowment of this gift, then, was conditioned upon his departure from earth to heaven. *It was to be his great ascension and coronation gift.* During the ages preceding his advent the Holy Ghost had been given in a measure. He had inspired the prophets; he had moved them to write and speak; he had testified within them the "sufferings of Christ and the glory which was to follow;" he had been imparted to the Baptist from his birth; and yet all this was not that great gift to the Church and the world which was to be imparted after his ascension and glorification. "The Holy Ghost was not yet [fully] given; because that Jesus was not glorified." John vii, 39. But now Jesus had gone away. They had seen him, reversing the laws of nature, ascending up toward heaven until a "cloud had received him out of their sight." He was no more with them in his bodily presence; but they *believed* what he had told them: "I ascend unto my Father, and your Father; and to my God, and your God." John xx, 17. How were they to *know* it? What evidence could they receive which would demonstrate the fact that he was "at the right hand of God exalted?" They no longer doubted his resurrection. The many "infallible signs" which he had given them of this had dissipated forever all their doubts and fears. Now how could they *know* that he was *glorified?* Christ himself had given the sign: "If I go away, I will send you another Comforter."

Let us illustrate this. Suppose you have a friend who is about to sail for India or China. Before his departure you converse with him, and he promises you, that if he shall arrive safely in the country to which he goes, he will write you a letter, and send you some of the peculiar productions of that country. The day arrives for his departure, and amid tears and farewells you watch the vessel until it disappears in the dim distance. You then return home, and wait in expectation of the promised letter and the promised gift. A few weeks pass away, and you begin to think the time is drawing near for the fulfillment of the promise, and you are on the anxious outlook for the mail carrier and the express-man; when, lo, on some bright morning a letter is handed you, and you see at a glance that the handwriting is that of your friend. What is the very first thought that enters your mind as you see it addressed from the country whither your friend has gone?

Why, you say, "No doubt he has arrived safely; he is certainly there." And when, a few hours later, the express-man arrives with a package containing the promised specimens, you are confirmed in your belief, and there is no further room for doubt. Now the disciples had seen their Lord and Master go into heaven. They stood gazing up into heaven as his chariot went up, until the angel voices startled them, and they turned to see them and listen to their words of hope and cheer. Then comes the period of waiting. They were not told *how long* they were to wait; but the assurance was given them that they should not wait long. "Ye shall be baptized with the Holy Ghost *not many days hence*." We have seen how they waited, and how they prayed, and how the promised gift was bestowed. And after the first outburst of their exuberant joy, what was the deep conviction, the undoubted assurance, which took possession of their hearts? Must they not joyfully and triumphantly have said to each other, "O, He is ascended! He is glorified! He is seated at the right hand of God the Father!" And how boldly did Peter declare this in his wonderful Pentecost sermon! "Therefore *being by the right hand of God exalted,* and having received of the Father the promise of the Holy Ghost, he hath shed forth this, which ye now see and hear." Acts ii, 33–36. With equal boldness did he testify before the Jewish Sanhedrim. "Him hath God exalted with his right hand to be a Prince and a Saviour, to give repentance to Israel, and forgiveness of sins. And we are his witnesses of these things; and so is also the Holy Ghost, whom God hath given to them that obey him." Acts v, 31, 32. Here, then, is the grand demonstration to the Church and the world of Christ's exaltation and mediation. O, there is not a sinner whose dark mind is illuminated with the light, and whose unbelieving heart is convinced by the power of the Holy Ghost, but who has an indubitable evidence that Christ is "seated at the right hand of God." And there is not a Christian who experiences the baptism of the Holy Ghost, but who knows as well that Jesus is glorified as if he had seen him with his own eyes sitting upon the eternal throne. So, when his peace and comfort and joy are imparted to the soul of the believer, he feels, he knows that he is exalted at God's right hand. Each repetition of the baptism increases the assurance, until "meridian evidence puts doubts to flight" forever.

> "*Enthroned* is Jesus now
>   Upon his heavenly seat;
> The kingly crown is on his brow;
>   The saints are at his feet."
>
> "*Enthroned* on high, Almighty Lord,
>   The Holy Ghost send down;
> Fulfill in us thy faithful word,
>   And all thy mercies crown."

CHAPTER IV.

THE FULL BESTOWMENT OF THE COMFORTER CONDITIONED UPON THE DEPARTURE OF CHRIST FROM THE WORLD.

"IT is *expedient* for you," said the Son of God, "that I go away: for if I go not away, *the Comforter will not come unto you; but if I depart, I will send him unto you.*" John xvi, 7. No language could have made it clearer to the minds of the disciples that, if the Comforter, who was to abide with them forever, came, Christ must depart from them. Why was this? Had not the Holy Ghost been given to men before this? And if so, how was this new coming to differ from all his former manifestations? There can be no doubt whatever that the Spirit had been given during each of the preceding dispensations; and, also, even during Christ's sojourn with his disciples. Far back, in the very dawn of the patriarchal dispensation, God had said, "My Spirit shall not always strive with man." Gen. vi, 3. He must, then, have been given at that very early period in order that he might strive with man. Again, St. Peter says, "Holy men of God spake as they were moved by the Holy Ghost." 2 Pet. i, 21. Of John the Baptist it was said, "He shall be filled with the Holy Ghost, even from his mother's womb." Luke i, 15. It was said of Elizabeth that she "was filled with the Holy Ghost." Luke i, 41, 67. The same is said of Zacharias. The aged Simeon, the Evangelist says, had "the Holy Ghost upon him." And it was revealed to him by the Holy Ghost that "he should not see death, before he had seen the Lord's Christ." Luke ii, 25, 26. It was by the Spirit, also, that he came into the temple. (Luke ii, 27.) Mary herself received the Holy Ghost, that she might become the mother of our Lord. (Luke i, 35.) Our Saviour, speaking to his disciples, says of the Spirit, "whom the world cannot receive, because it seeth him not, neither knoweth him: but ye know him; for he *dwelleth with you,* and shall be in you." John xiv, 17.

And yet, notwithstanding these frequent references, it is expressly declared by the Evangelist, "The Holy Ghost was not yet given; because that Jesus was not yet glorified." John vii, 39. How, then, are these statements to be reconciled? The only solution of this difficulty is that, until the ascension and glorification of Christ, the Spirit was only *partially* and *temporarily* given ; while since his exaltation to the right hand of God he has been fully and constantly poured forth. There were only certain offices, which, previous to Christ's exaltation, the Spirit had exercised. He had striven with the antediluvians. He had inspired the prophets, and Mary, Elizabeth, Zachariah, Simeon, Anna, and John the Baptist. In a measure, he had dwelt with the disciples. But all will readily perceive how limited and transient were his gifts. His most glorious manifestation under the Old Testament dispensation was as "the spirit of prophecy." In this high and glorious office he had opened the eyes of the prophets, so that they could look down the vistas of the ages, and see the rise and fall of empires, kingdoms, and states, and, especially, the coming and glory of the kingdom of the Messiah. Inspired by his presence and power, their souls had been kindled into rapture, and made to glow with ecstasies divine. They had been transported beyond themselves, and, rapt in the visions of God, they had uttered truths which they could never have reasoned out or known; had used words which they could not have used; and had poured forth the most magnificent poetic effusions which have held the ages enraptured and entranced. And yet this gift was not *always* upon them, it was not *abiding*. And when the Divine Afflatus departed they were weak, and feeble, and ignorant as other men. But for the time being, while the Spirit was upon them, "They were," says an eloquent writer,* "a momentary incarnation—a meteor, kindled at the eye, and blown on the breath, of the Eternal." To the ancient prophet, then, the Holy Ghost was an occasional visitant, mighty in his operations, and glorious in his manifestations. Suddenly He came upon him, and as suddenly departed. Sometimes returning at different periods, and in other cases, probably, only realized once in the whole lifetime of the man of God. Various, also, were the means he employed in revealing himself to the prophets, sometimes speaking to them in dreams and visions of the night, when his conscious presence would make their hair to stand up and their flesh to crawl. Then again, after periods of fasting and prayer, on the banks of

* Gilfillan.

the Ulai, the Chebar, or the Euphrates. Thus, as the apostle says, "at sundry times and in divers manners God spake unto the fathers by the prophets." Heb. i, 1. But there is no evidence whatever that he was given to the Church, in these former dispensations, as he was given at the day of Pentecost, or as he is now given to believers. The prophets themselves were made conscious that a brighter and more glorious dispensation was to follow their own. Hence, the frequency with which they speak of "*that day.*" They saw the coming on of that day; they anxiously desired to see the day itself; but they only saw it in the distant future. The Prophet Joel speaks of this wonderful and universal outpouring of the Spirit as occurring "in the last days." And when the Apostle Peter stood up on the day in which the Church received the mighty baptism, he said, "This *is* that which was spoken by the Prophet Joel." It was, indeed, the grand fulfillment of the ancient prophecies, the blessed realization of the Saviour's promise. Now Jesus had departed Now he was glorified at the right hand of God. Now the Comforter had come, as it had been foretold and fore-promised. And now, too, *he had come to stay*—to stay "until the redemption of the purchased possession," and until the final "restitution of all things." But he had come to give, not always the power of working miracles, or of speaking with tongues, but to be the great enlightener, regenerator, and sanctifier of the race. Now the Spirit is to be so in the heart of the believer, that out of it should "flow rivers of living water." John vii, 38. Calvin's exposition of this promise is very fine. He says, "Christ here teaches the abundant fullness to be found in him, which will refresh us to satiety. It is, indeed, a rather strong metaphor when rivers of living water are said to flow out of the hearts of believers. Nevertheless, the sense is by no means doubtful, namely, that no spiritual blessing shall ever be wanting to them that believe. *Rivers*, in the plural number, I understand to express the multiplied graces of the Spirit which are necessary to the spiritual life of the soul. In short, here is promised to us the perpetuity of the gifts of the Spirit, as well as their abundance. But we are also admonished by this how small may be the measure of our faith when the Spirit barely distills upon us, drop by drop, that which might flow like a river, if we would give the right place to Christ; that is, should our faith render us capable of receiving him."

But the question now arises, Why was it necessary that Christ should depart in order to the full bestowment of the Spirit? To this I answer, first, It was essential in order that the apostles and Christians in all ages might learn to *walk by faith.* Paul expressly declares, "We walk by faith, not by sight." 2 Cor. v, 7. And they thus walked because God had given unto them "the earnest of the Spirit." 2 Cor. v, 5. In view of this he sums up the whole argument by saying, "Wherefore, henceforth know we no man after the flesh: yea, though we have known Christ after the flesh, yet now henceforth know we him no more." 2 Cor. v, 16.

Christ had been with them for three years. He had called them his "brethren," his "friends." They had heard his voice, had seen him with their own eyes; they had looked upon him, and their hands had handled "the Word of life." 1 John i, 1. In all their doubts and difficulties they had gone directly to him, and they were not satisfied unless they were in his immediate presence. And when he had spoken to them of going away sorrow had filled their hearts. We all know that upon the Mount of Transfiguration Peter had wanted to build three tabernacles, so that their Master might abide with them there. Thus they were walking almost wholly by *sight,* gazing with wondering eyes upon the Saviour's miracles, or listening with admiration and awe to his unearthly teachings, although failing often to understand their great import. His visible and tangible presence seemed to be more and more necessary to them the longer he remained with them. They had come, in some instances at least, to regard that his actual presence was essential to the performance of his mighty works. It was so with both Mary and Martha. Much as they loved him, cordially as they embraced him as the promised Messiah, yet they evidently had this idea when each of them said, "Lord, if thou hadst been *here* my brother had not died." John xi, 21, 32. Just as if his visible presence was essential to the restoration of their brother. But it was the design of Christ that the new dispensation should not be sensuous but spiritual—not one which should appeal to the eye, but one which should engage the confidence and the affections of the heart. Hence, after his resurrection, Christ said to the once doubting, but now overwhelmingly convinced, Thomas, "Because thou hast seen me, thou hast believed: blessed are they that have not seen, and yet have believed." John xx, 29. So the Apostle Peter says, "Whom *having not seen,* ye love; in whom, though now ye see him not, yet believing, ye rejoice with joy unspeakable and full of glory." 1 Peter i, 8. But then, if they, in a still higher and sublimer sense than Moses did, were to "endure as seeing Him who is invisible," they must be sustained by a faith which is inspired by the Holy Spirit. That they might "walk by faith and not by sight," Jesus was taken away from them, and that this faith might be inspired and maintained the Spirit was given to them.

2. His departure was essential not only to a life of faith, but also that our love to him might be *spiritual and divine, and not fleshly and human.* There was a tradition among the Jewish people that Christ, when he came, would never die. This is evident from their language to him when he had spoken to them of his being

"lifted up," which they evidently understood, as he intended they should understand him, namely, as "signifying by what death he should die." "We have heard," say they, "out of the law that Christ abideth forever: and how sayest thou, The Son of man must be lifted up?" John xii, 31–34. So when he spoke to his disciples of his sufferings and death, Peter said, "Be it far from thee, Lord: this shall not be unto thee." Matt. xvi, 22. Such was their love for his person, that any mention of his departure from them filled them with amazement and grief. Thus it is evident that their love for him, while, doubtless, it was ardent and sincere, yet was not as pure and spiritual as it was after they received the Spirit. St. Augustine says, "It seems to me that the disciples had been occupied with the human form of our Lord Jesus Christ, and, being men, were controlled, as it were, by human affection to man. But he desired them rather to have a divine affection, and to be made spiritual instead of carnal, which a man does not become except by the gift of the Holy Spirit. This, therefore, he says, 'I send to you a gift by which you may be made spiritual, namely, the gift of the Holy

Spirit. You cannot become spiritual unless you cease to be carnal. Now you will cease to be carnal if the bodily form is withdrawn from your eyes, that the image of God may be placed in your hearts.' For by this human form the heart even of Peter was detained when he feared that he whom he loved much would die; for he loved the Lord Jesus Christ as a man loves man, as the carnal loves the carnal, not as the spiritual loves true majesty."

Let me suggest just here, that it has often seemed to me to be a relic of this human love when the expressions, "sweet Jesus," "dear Jesus," and the like are made use of. Without for a moment doubting the piety or the sincerity of many of those who habitually make use of such expressions in addressing Christ or speaking of him, at the same time I would express a sincere doubt as to the propriety and the profit of making use of them. The apostles of our Lord never speak thus of him, nor is there any evidence that the early Church employed this language. The same, and even greater, objections lie against the use of all images of Christ, or all attempts to form images of him in "the chambers of imagery," that we may humanly love and embrace him. This is one of the great errors of the Romish Church, and perhaps the very secret of her sensuous worship. On this point Archdeacon Hare says,* "But true it is that, while it is the glory of the Church of Rome to have preserved the confession of Christ, the Son of the living God, through so many ages, notwithstanding the open assaults and insidious snares of numberless forms of heresy, that Church has ever been especially apt to lose sight of the spiritual and divine truth in the outward human form. She has been unable to recognize how indeed it was expedient for Christ to go away. She has never been content unless she could get something present—a vicar, images, outward works, actual sacrifices, with priests to offer them up, real flesh and real blood. She chose rather to defy the evidence of the senses than not to have an object of sense." And Calvin in his Commentary on the text, "It is expedient for you that I go away," etc., says, "Because we are carnal, nothing is more difficult than to tear from our minds this preposterous affection, by which we draw Christ to us from heaven." It is the sturdy, brawny

* Mission of the Comforter, p. 234.

faith of the soul which is more enlightened and sanctified, which eliminates from it the earthly, the groveling, and the human, and soars aloft into the sublimer altitudes of love divine. It is true that his human soul and his human body ally him and endear him to our humanity, but we are to know him, and to love him after the flesh, no more.

3. His departure was necessary in order that his disciples and his Church might be "*led into all truth.*" It was his own promise that "When He, the Spirit of truth, shall come, he shall guide you into all truth"—*πᾶσαν τῆν ἀλήθείαν*, all *the* truth. "He shall not speak of himself; but whatsoever he shall hear, that shall he speak." John xvi, 13. "He shall testify of *me.*" John xv, 26. When Christ was with them he told them that he had yet many things to say to them, but that they "could not bear them then." John xvi, 12. And we all know that while Christ was with them they were very slow of heart to understand what he said to them. There seemed to be a mist, a vail upon their minds. All that he said to them about his death, his resurrection and ascension, they did not seem to comprehend. But the promise was, that the Spirit should guide them

into all the truth. I understand by this that they should be guided by him, not into all scientific, or purely speculative truth, but the truth as it is in Jesus—"the truth as it relates to man's present and eternal well-being." Hence we see that, as soon as the Spirit was given to them, they seem to have had a new revelation of Christ. He was no longer to them merely "the man Christ Jesus," "Jesus of Nazareth," or a man of poverty, sorrow, and grief; but "exalted to the right hand of God," "a Prince and a Saviour," "The Son of God," "God over all, blessed forever!" "He was no longer a mere teacher and example, but transfigured into their God and Saviour and Redeemer." * They had, as we have seen, the clearest evidence of his resurrection; they now had the most undoubting faith in his Godhead. "The history of the disciples, of the light they received, and of what they did after the ascension and the outpouring of the Holy Ghost, explains and confirms our Lord's words. None but he who had been crucified, had risen, and been glorified—the Son of God, who sat at the right hand of the Father—could be preached by the apostles as the

* Hare, p. 55.

Saviour of the whole world, and as the Lord of a new eternal and spiritual kingdom of heaven. None but the Son of God, who had overcome death, and returned in triumph to the Father, could the Paraclete proclaim to the world as the fulfiller of all righteousness, as the conqueror of the prince of this world, and as him unbelief in whom is sin." * So Augustine says: "It was necessary that the servant form should be removed from their eyes, because they thought this alone, which they saw, to be Christ. Hence his word: 'If ye loved me, ye would rejoice, because I go unto, the Father; for my Father is greater than I;' that is, It is necessary for me to go to the Father, because, while ye thus behold me ye judge, from what ye see, that I am less than the Father, and, occupied with my created and assumed nature, ye do not perceive the equality which I have with the Father. Hence also the language, 'Touch me not; for I am not yet ascended to my Father.' For touch makes an end, as it were, to conception. And he was unwilling that what was seen should be thought the whole, that the heart directed to him should pause with the visible. By ascend-

* Locke.

ing to the Father he was to appear as equal to the Father."

Peter, and the other disciples, had caught occasional glimpses of this great truth. They had stood in awe and amazement at his wonderful power, when he had commanded the winds and the sea, and they had obeyed him. But even then they had asked, "What manner of *man* is this?" Matt. viii, 27. When the miraculous draught of fishes had been secured, Peter had fallen down at the feet of his Master, overwhelmed by a sense of his wisdom and his power, and had said, "Depart from me; for I am a sinful man, O Lord." Luke v, 8. And then, too, when Jesus asked his disciples, "Whom say *ye* that I am?" Peter, answering for himself and the other disciples, said, "Thou art the Christ, the Son of the living God." Matt. xvi, 16. This answer was given, however, under the influence of a direct revelation from God: "Blessed art thou, Simon Bar-Jona: for flesh and blood hath not revealed it unto thee, but my Father which is in heaven." Matt. xvi, 17. But not always was the mind of Peter so clear in its conceptions of the character of his Master. If he had continued to believe this, would he have *denied* his Lord "with oaths and curses?" No, indeed. But when he saw him standing a prisoner at the bar, and the whole power of the Jewish hierarchy threatening his death, his faith gave way under the pressure, and he fell fearfully into sin. True, his great brawny, noble heart was broken, and he wept bitterly when his Lord *looked* upon him; but then, again, his death seems to have extinguished all hope within his breast. There is great significance in his saying to the other disciples, "I go a fishing," and in their answer, "We also go with thee." John xxi, 3. They knew not how they were to be employed, and hence they returned to their former means of obtaining a livelihood.

But after the descent of the Holy Ghost upon them, they never doubted the divine character of their Lord. With the utmost boldness they preached "Jesus and the resurrection" in the very face of imprisonment, torture, and death. Besides this, the whole character of the sufferings and death, the resurrection and ascension, as well as the way of salvation by faith in his blood, seems to have burst at once upon their minds. The complete fulfillment of ancient prophecies and promises, the grand antetypal and substantial completement of the sacrifices of the law in Christ, all were brought out clearly to their minds. The whole Levitical priesthood and economy, and all the writings of the old prophets, were luminous, and all aglow, under the influence of the mighty baptism of the Spirit which was upon them. Thus the entire rounds of Christian doctrine, recorded in the Gospels and the Epistles, and embraced by all true believers for nearly two thousand years, loomed up "with all its rays complete" before their astonished minds.

5. *His departure was essential to the universal spread of the Gospel.* It was hardly possible for the Gospel to travel out into the regions beyond Judea while our Lord remained upon the earth. His presence with his disciples *localized* all their ideas of his operations and of his kingdom, and confined their labors to the narrow limits of the Holy Land. His command to the seventy had, indeed, positively restricted their labors to the Jews alone. But his post-resurrection command was extended to "all the world," and "to every creature." Mark xvi, 15. This command was based upon, and derived all its authority and emphasis from, the all-power which was given him in heaven

and earth. (Matt. xxviii, 18.) And in harmony with the command was the promise, "Lo, I am with you alway, even unto the end of the world." Matt. xxviii, 20. And the further one, "Ye shall receive power, after that the Holy Ghost is come upon you: and ye shall be witnesses unto me both in Jerusalem, and in all Judea, and in Samaria, and *unto the uttermost part of the earth.*" Acts i, 8.

"Not till he was taken away from them did they learn to feel that He was with them not merely in Judea, but in every part of the world. So long as he was living upon earth he might give light to the country round, like a beacon upon a hill. But it was only from his sun-like throne in the heavens that he could pour light over every quarter of the globe. It was only from thence that his voice could go forth throughout all the earth, and his words unto the end of the world. It was only when he was lifted up that he could draw all men to his feet. Then alone could the foundations of his Church be laid so deep and wide that all nations could be gathered into it."*

To the same effect Bishop Andrews says, "As the disciples were to be sent abroad into

* Hare, p. 46.

all coasts, to be scattered all over the earth to preach the Gospel, and not to stay together still in one place, Christ's corporal presence would have stood them in small stead. He could have been resident but in one place, to have comforted some one of them, St. James at Jerusalem: as for John at Ephesus, or Thomas in India, or Peter at Babylon—as good for them in heaven as in earth; all one. The Spirit which was to succeed was much more fit for men dispersed. He could be, and was present with them all, and with every one by himself, as filling the compass of the whole world."* There is peculiar significance here in the promise, "Lo, I am with you alway, even unto the end of the world." In his bodily presence this could not have been verified; he could not have been with each of them always and every-where; but by his Spirit the promise has been faithfully and gloriously fulfilled to the joy and comfort of all the laborers in his vineyard. Wherever his servants have gone preaching the Gospel, whether among "Barbarians, Scythians, bond or free;" amid hyperborean regions of eternal ice and snow, or amid the burning heats of tropical

* Sermons on sending the Holy Ghost.

regions, every-where his presence has been realized through the agency of the Eternal Spirit. His departure, and the consequent coming of the Comforter, were essential, also, to break down the middle wall of partition between the Jews and Gentiles. Thus the mighty barriers of the ages were removed. So strong had been the prejudices of the disciples, that it required a miraculous interposition, and a special command of the Spirit to Peter, to induce him to go to the house of Cornelius. Nor was it until he had preached unto the family and friends of the Centurion, and the Spirit had fallen upon them as upon the disciples at the beginning, that the truth burst fully upon his mind that redemption was provided for them. So the Church at Jerusalem, still encased in the bigoted prejudices of Judaism, contended with Peter because he had gone to men uncircumcised, and had eaten with them. (Acts xi, 3.) But when he had "rehearsed the matter from the beginning," and had told them how "the Holy Ghost fell on them, as on us at the beginning, . . . they held their peace, and glorified God, saying, Then hath God also to the Gentiles granted repentance unto life." Acts xi, 4, 15, 18.

It was thus, and by the persecution which scattered the members of the Jerusalem Church, that the sacred fire, which had been pent up in the Holy City and in Judea, now overleaped these narrow boundaries, and spread in every direction, until the world's cold heart began to melt under its power, and its darkness fled before the brilliancy of its radiance. Hence we see that the departure of Christ was essential to the full bestowment of his Spirit, and the universal extension of his kingdom.

CHAPTER V.

THE GIFT OF THE COMFORTER—WHAT IT COMPRISES.

JESUS is glorified. The Holy Ghost is given. Let us, then, fix our gaze upon the character and importance of the gift which we have received. What, then, does this gift comprise? As we look at the gift, and endeavor to appreciate its richness, its freeness and fullness—its infinite variety of blessings—we are, we must be, overwhelmed with its greatness. And yet how slow have we been to appreciate its value and importance! How often has it been undesired and unsought; yea, how often has it been despised, resisted, and refused? O, wonder of wonders, that such a gift should be offered to us on the simple condition of asking for it, and yet that we are so slow to ask, and so unwilling to receive it! But now let us endeavor to understand the gift so freely promised, so freely bestowed. The blessed Comforter, the ascension gift of Jesus, comes to us himself, bringing the richest gifts. The early Church was flooded with these gifts—both in their extraordinary and ordinary forms. The apostle enumerates them as follows: "Now there are diversities of gifts, but the same Spirit. . . . But the manifestation of the Spirit is given to every man to profit withal. For to one is given by the Spirit the word of wisdom; to another the word of knowledge by the same Spirit; to another faith by the same Spirit; to another the gifts of healing by the same Spirit; to another the working of miracles; to another prophecy; to another discerning of spirits; to another divers kinds of tongues; to another the interpretation of tongues: but all these worketh that one and the self-same Spirit, dividing to every man severally as he will." 1 Cor. xii, 4, 7–11. So also in verses 28–30: "And God hath set some in the church, first apostles, secondarily prophets, thirdly teachers, after that miracles, then gifts of healings, helps, governments, diversities of tongues." But he adds, "Are all apostles? are all prophets? are all teachers? are all workers of miracles? have all the gifts of healing? do all speak with tongues?" In Rom. xii, 6–8, we have anothother division of these gifts: "Having then gifts differing according to the grace that is given to us, whether prophecy, let us prophesy according to the proportion of faith; or ministry, let us wait on our ministering; or he that teacheth, on teaching; or he that exhorteth, on exhortation." So in Eph. iv, 11, 12, "And he gave some, apostles; and some, prophets; and some, evangelists; and some, pastors and teachers; for the perfecting of the saints, for the work of the ministry, for the edifying of the body of Christ."

The following classification of these gifts has been made, and as it serves so clearly to impress them upon the mind, I quote it entire:

I.

1 Cor. xii, 8.

CLASS I—ῳ μὲν.	CLASS II—ἑτέρῳ δὲ.	CLASS III—ἑτέρῳ δὲ
1. λόγος σοφίας, *Word of wisdom.*	1. πίστις, *Faith.*	1. γένε γλωσσῶν, *Divers kinds of tongues.*
2. λόγος γνώσεως, *Word of knowledge.*	2. χαρίσματα ἰαμάτων *Gifts of healing.*	2. ἑρμηνεία γλωσσων, *Interpretation of tongues.*
	3. ἐνεργήματα δυνάμεων, *Working of miracles.*	
	4. προφητεία, *Prophecy.*	
	5. διακρίσεις πνευμάτων, *Discerning of spirits.*	

II.

1 Cor. xii, 28.

1. ἀπόστολοί, *Apostles.*
2. προφῆται, *Prophets.* (See 4 in Class II.)
3. διδάσκαλοι, *Teachers.* (Including 1 and 2 in Class I, and perhaps)
4. δυνάμεις, *Miracles.* (See 3 in Class II.)
1. χαρίσματα ἰαμάτων, *Gifts of healing.* (See 2 of Class II.)
2. ἀντιλήψεις, *Helps.*
3. Κυβερνήσεις, *Governments.*
4. γένη γλωσσῶν, *Diversities of tongues.* (See 1 of Class 3.)*

But nearly all, if not all these gifts were extraordinary in their character, and limited as to the period of their bestowment. Nor did every member of the early Church enjoy *all* these gifts. All were not even then "apostles," all were not prophets, nor teachers, nor workers of miracles. There are, however, gifts of the Spirit which have been denominated "ordinary," that is, which it is the privilege of every child of God in every age to enjoy. And, also, there are gifts which this redeemed world will possess until the consummation of all things. Such are his gifts of enlightenment and conviction to the world, of regeneration, the witness of adoption, and the entire sanctification of the believer.

* Howson and Conybeare, Life and Epistles of St. Paul, vol. i., pp., 427, 428. Note.

Such are also the fruits of his indwelling and his grace—"Love, joy, peace, long-suffering, gentleness, goodness, faith, meekness, temperance." Gal. v, 22, 23. The first of these is the common heritage of humanity, and the second is the common heritage of the people of God; they have been enjoyed by the Church from the day of Pentecost until now, and they will continue in it until the end of time. Nor has the Church, notwithstanding the apparent limitations of them, been *entirely* destitute of the extraordinary gifts of the Spirit. I would not be considered as referring with any degree of favor to the mania of the Irvingites of England, who claimed to speak in "unknown tongues." Indeed, they were "unknown." They neither knew them themselves, nor did any living man know them. Their utterances were nothing but unintelligible jargon. Nor do I regard as worthy of serious notice the claims of the Elders of the Mormon Church to speak with tongues, and to perform miraculous works. Whatever of gibberish these poor deluded creatures indulge in, it certainly is not the speaking with tongues which characterized the apostolic age. Nor have they ever been able to substantiate a claim to the working of a genuine miracle.

I do not say that the power to work miracles will *never* again be given to the Church. There is certainly no authority for believing or saying this. All that we know on this subject is the historical fact that the power to work miracles *seems* to have been limited to apostolic days. But, as a certain writer well says, "Miracles were as the tolling of the great bell of the universe to call the attention of mankind to the service. When the service has commenced the bell stops; but it may ring out again when the service is over, and the congregation is going home." How do we know but that the Holy Ghost may yet endow his ministers with this wondrous power? What I would now, however, particularly refer to is the fact that there have been, in the history of the Church, instances of extraordinary faith, produced by the Holy Spirit, which have been marked by extraordinary manifestations and results. There are instances in the life of Bramwell, of Pastor John Bort and his wife of the Department of Dordogna, in France, of Father Zeller of Bruggen, in the Grand Duchy of Baden, and of Müller, in Bristol, England, which are supernatural and superhuman. I ask, Is not the faith exhibited by these persons extraordinary? Have *all* Christians had this gift? Do *all* Christians have it? Furthermore, is it not the work of the Spirit to produce such a faith? And when such a faith has been, and is exercised, is not God pleased to own and honor it? Yet, again, are we not warranted to expect that in the last days there will be more extraordinary manifestations of the Spirit than any which the Church or the world have ever before witnessed? I think so. What marvels or miracles may accompany such visitations I cannot tell. One thing, however, is certain, that the Church scarcely yet conceives the wondrous power which she may realize and wield for her grand triumph in the world. Ay, and we have scarcely more than tasted of the fullness of the baptism of the Spirit—of his love, his light, his power, his peace, and his joy. O that our eyes may be opened to see the fullness of the promise! O that our hearts may be opened to embrace the promises, and to know experimentally their fullness and their power!

There can be no doubt, then, that, long as this

dispensation lasts, the ungodly will have the illumination, the reproof, the conviction and the call of the Spirit unconditionally bestowed through the mediation of Jesus Christ, and that the believer will have the renewing power, the conscious witness of his forgiveness, his justification and adoption, and the sealing and sanctifying grace of the Holy Spirit. Ay, more: that he shall be endued with his power to witness for Christ, and be filled with the peace and joy and hope which he imparts. Never will these gifts be withdrawn from the Church or the world ; but we may expect that they will be enjoyed in greater fullness and in richer abundance as we approach the glories of the millennial period.

CHAPTER VI.

THE COMFORTER THE SOURCE OF THE INSPIRATION OF THE SCRIPTURES.

IF the Bible is indeed the word of God, as it purports to be, then it is the product of the inspiration of the Holy Ghost. If it is not the word of God, then it is the word of man, and, as such, has no claim upon the credence or confidence of intelligent beings. And more than this; the writers of these books uniformly and unequivocally declare that they wrote and spoke at the dictate and under the inspiration of God. If, therefore, it could be ascertained that they were either deceivers or deceived, then their writings would be nothing but a tissue of falsehood and deceit. I can see no alternative. The writers of these books were what they professed to be—God-inspired men—or they were vile impostors, and deserve the reprobation of mankind. Here are sixty-six books, written during the progress of sixteen centuries by men of various conditions and circumstances—from the humble shepherd to the great lawgiver, from the peasant to the monarch, from the unlettered fisherman to the learned and logical Paul—and yet all agree in their teaching of the character and will of God, the redemption of man, and a future state.

Here, in this wondrous book, are history and poetry, narrative and description, prophecy and promise, at times rising to the most exalted strains of eloquence unequaled in all the literature of this world, and then again falling to the simple record of genealogies, the familiar parable, or the unvarnished narrative; but all so wonderfully blended, so harmoniously wrought, that, like an inimitable mosaic, they exhibit only one plan or design. Of no human productions can this be said.

Then, again, there never has been a book which has been called to pass through such an ordeal as this. It has been in the fiery crucible of criticism, investigation, and persecution for centuries gone by. The most acute minds, some animated by bitterest prejudice and hate, others sincere and honest inquirers after truth, have with the utmost scrutiny examined every book, every chapter, every verse, every sentence, and every word of this book. The history of nations, their arts and sciences, their customs and manners, their topography, hieroglyphics, entablatures, coins, their philosophics and their poetry, the exhumation of buried cities—all have been ransacked, or unraveled, or deciphered, to confirm or disprove its records. Every new development of science has been, and still is, seized upon with the utmost avidity to ascertain if some fact or principle could not be evoked from it which would undermine or disprove the statements of this book. And yet, while not professing to teach science, and while adapting its references to it to the actual conditions of the times in which its books were written, nothing has yet been settled upon or fixed in science, in all its developments, during all the procession of the centuries, which in any sense conflicts with it. It is well known that in the early history of the sciences of astronomy, chemistry, and, later, of geology, men have supposed that they had found unmistakable evidences of the falsity of the records of the Bible; but subsequent investigation has demonstrated how utterly futile all such hasty conclusions and premature announcements were. And thus it must ever continue to be. The reason for this is obvious. The author and inspirer of this book is the same Almighty Spirit who erst moved upon the face of the mighty deep, bringing order out of disorder, and who garnished the heavens with beauty and glory. Look now at the fact,

1. *That this book claims to be inspired.*—"*All* Scripture is given by inspiration of God, and is profitable for doctrine, for reproof, for correction, for instruction in righteousness." 2 Tim. iii, 16. "For the prophecy came not in old time by the will of man: but holy men of God spake as they were moved by the Holy Ghost." 2 Pet. i, 21. "Searching what, or what manner of time the Spirit of Christ which was in them did signify, when it testified beforehand the sufferings of Christ, and the glory that should follow." 1 Pet. i, 11. All those prophecies then in the Old Testament Scriptures which speak of the sufferings of Christ, and the glory following those sufferings, were testified to and written under the influence of the Spirit of Christ which was in the ancient prophets. Our Saviour teaches us that David was inspired when he wrote Psalm cx: "How then doth David in spirit

[mark, by the Holy Ghost, that is, by his inspiration] call him [Christ] Lord ?" Matt. xxii, 43. St. Paul affirms the inspiration of Isaiah when he says, "Well *spake the Holy Ghost* by Esaias the prophet unto our fathers." Acts xxviii, 25. He also clearly announces the inspiration of David the Psalmist in Psalm xcv: "Wherefore as the *Holy Ghost saith.*" Heb. iii, 7. The Lord Jesus Christ puts the seal of his own acknowledgment and authority upon Moses, the prophets and the Psalms. (Luke xxiv, 44.) The apostles of our Lord were promised the same Spirit: "But the Comforter, which is the Holy Ghost, whom the Father will send in my name, he shall teach you all things, and bring all things to your remembrance, whatsoever I have said unto you." John xiv, 26.

Well does a recent writer say, "But *whose* design is this, which appears not in the separate books, but in the collection taken as a whole? The agents were severed from each other, and wrote as their respective terms of mind and historical circumstances determined. Where, then, was the presiding mind which planned the whole, and, in qualifying and employing the chosen agents, divided to every man severally as he would? By the voice of the Church as a body, by the ever-accumulating consent of her several members, an unchanging answer comes down from age to age. The Spirit of the Lord is here.

"Yes, the Spirit was to testify of Jesus, and the fourfold Gospel is his permanent testimony." *

2. The writers of these books in nearly every instance directly announce that they wrote and spoke under this inspiration. Their predictions and statements are not made in their own names, or by their own authority, but it is uniformly declared as "Thus saith the Lord." We have seen the authoritative sanction which Christ and his apostles have given to Moses, David, and the prophets, and the especial declaration of the inspiration of David and Isaiah. Let us see now how they speak of themselves and their writings. Moses frequently said to the children of Israel, "These are the words of the Lord your God." And the law which he brought down from Sinai he declared was "written with the finger of God." Deut. ix, 10. Jere-

* Bernard's Progress of Doctrine in the New Testament, pp. 72, 73.

miah says that "the word of the Lord came to nim." "Then the Lord put forth his hand, and touched my mouth. And the Lord said unto me, Behold, I have put my words in thy mouth." Jer. i, 2, 9. Ezekiel says, "The word of the Lord came expressly unto" him. Ezek. i, 3. Again, nearly every chapter begins as follows: "The word of the Lord came unto me." Daniel attributes his power to interpret dreams, and the visions which he had of the future, to the wisdom and power of God. (Dan. ii, 19–23, 27, 28.) Nebuchadnezzar was made aware of this fact, and acknowledged it in his proclamation. (Dan. iv, 9.) The wife of Belshazzar evidently understood the same. (Dan. v, 11.) Daniel also assures us that he was able to understand the import of some of his own prophetical utterances and of his wonderful visions only by the intervention of an angel commissioned by God for this purpose. (Dan. viii, 16; ix, 21, 22; x, 11.)

Hosea says, "The word of the Lord came" to him, (Hos. i, 1,) and all his announcements are made as from the Lord. It is the same with Joel, Amos, Obadiah, Jonah, Micah, Nahum, Habakkuk, Zephaniah, Zechariah, and Malachi.

The proof of the inspiration of the New Testament Scriptures is equally clear and positive. In the first place the Lord Jesus Christ expressly promised the Holy Ghost to his apostles for the purpose of enabling them to remember all he had said to them, and of guiding them into all truth. "But the Comforter, which is the Holy Ghost, whom the Father will send in my name, he shall teach you all things, and bring all things to your remembrance, whatsoever I have said unto you." John xiv, 26.

"But when the Comforter is come, whom I will send unto you from the Father, even the Spirit of truth, which proceedeth from the Father, he shall testify of me: and ye also shall bear witness, because ye have been with me from the beginning." John xv, 26, 27. "Howbeit when he, the Spirit of truth, is come, he will guide you into all [the] truth: . . . and he will show you things to come. He shall glorify me: for he shall receive of mine, and shall show it unto you." John xvi, 13, 14. The evidence upon this point is so clear and explicit that argument is unneeded. In addition to this, the apostles and evangelists themselves claim to have written and spoken under the direct inspiration of the Holy Ghost. On the day of Pentecost the promised baptism of the Holy Ghost came upon the disciples, and, as the result of that baptism, they "began to speak with other tongues, as the Spirit gave them utterance." Acts ii, 4. And what did they thus speak? Those who heard them bore testimony as follows: "We do hear them speak in our tongues the wonderful works of God." Acts ii, 11. The Apostle Paul in a number of instances claims this inspiration for himself and his co-apostles. "But we speak the wisdom of God in a mystery, even the hidden wisdom, which God ordained before the world unto our glory." "Eye hath not seen, nor ear heard, neither have entered into the heart of man, the things which God hath prepared for them that love him. But God hath revealed them unto us by his spirit: . . . Now we have received, not the spirit of the world, but the spirit which is of God; that we might know the things that are freely given to us of God. Which things also we speak, not in the words which man's wisdom teacheth, but which the Holy Ghost teacheth; comparing spiritual things with spiritual"—that is, explaining spiritual things in spiritual words.* (1 Cor. ii, 9, 10, 12, 13.)

In his Epistle to the Galatians he says, "I certify you, brethren, that the Gospel which was preached by me was not after man. For I neither received it of man, neither was I taught it, but by the revelation of Jesus Christ." Gal. i, 11, 12. "But when it pleased God to reveal his Son in me, that I might preach him among the heathen." Gal. i, 15, 16. Once more, "If any man think himself to be a prophet, or spiritual, let him acknowledge the things which I write unto you are the commandments of the Lord." 1 Cor. xiv, 37. It is needless to quote further, although, as Dr. Dwight says, "In near two hundred different passages, in one manner and another, St. Paul asserts explicitly the inspiration of himself and his companions in the Gospel." † But not only so. The apostles claim that the Gospel which they preached is "the Gospel of God," "the Gospel of Christ," "the power of God unto salvation;" that where it is believed, "it is the savor of life unto life," and where it is rejected, "it is the savor of death unto death;" and, finally, that "if any man,

* Dr. Macknight. † Theology, vol. ii, p. 128.

or if any angel, preach another Gospel, let him be accursed." Then the whole New Testament canon is closed by these words of solemn warning and threatening: "If any man shall add unto these words, God shall add unto him the plagues that are written in this book: and if any man shall take away from the words of the book of this prophecy, God shall take away his part out of the book of life, and out of the holy city, and from the things which are written in this book." Rev. xxii, 18, 19.

Furthermore, in confirmation of that Gospel which they preached, miracles, signs, and wonders were wrought by God through them. But would God work miracles to attest false or spurious doctrines? Yea, is it to be supposed that he would work miracles to support a merely human opinion? Was not the very design of his working these miracles to confirm the word spoken by the apostles, and to show to those who heard them that it was, indeed, his own word? Is not the very idea that he would work miracles to support a falsehood blasphemous? And if the apostles were *not* inspired of God to write and speak as they did, then they were deceivers, and their utterances were false. Let us hear what they say on this subject: "And they went forth and preached every-where; the Lord working with them, and confirming the word with signs [miracles] following." Mark xvi, 20.

So St. Paul says: "How shall we escape, if we neglect so great salvation; which at the first began to be spoken by the Lord, and was confirmed unto us by those that heard him; God also bearing them witness, both with signs and wonders, and with divers miracles, and gifts of the Holy Ghost, according to his own will?" Heb. ii, 3, 4. It is scarcely necessary to add that these truths and asseverations in reference to the source whence they were derived were uttered in the very midst of the severest persecutions, privations, and perils; and, finally, they sealed them with their own blood, thus giving the clearest and the highest evidence which they were capable of giving of their sincerity, their truthfulness, and their title to our credence.

3. With equal clearness do the writers of the word of God claim that not only the *substance* of what they wrote was revealed unto them, but also that the *very words* in which they originally

wrote these books were also directly from God. This position, of course, does not cover the blunders or biases of translators, the carelessness and mistakes of copyists, or the fallibility and weakness of interpreters; but it does cover all that "holy men of old," whether prophets, apostles, or evangelists, "wrote and spoke." While it comes not within the province of this volume to enter largely into the discussion of this question, yet I may be permitted to present the two leading views held by the Christian world on this subject. The first I will speak of is that which regards this inspiration as *plenary*. It is thus presented by an able commentator of the present day: "The inspiration of the sacred writers I believe to have consisted in the fullness of the influence of the Holy Spirit, especially raising them to, and enabling them for, their work, *in a manner which distinguishes them from all other writers in the world, and their work from all other works.* The men were full of the Holy Ghost; the books are the pouring out of that fullness through the men, the conservation of the treasure in earthen vessels. The treasure is ours in all its richness; but it is ours, as only it can be ours, in the imperfections of human speech, in the limitations of human thought, in the variety incident at first to individual character, and then to manifold transcription and the lapse of ages."* On the other hand, many very able writers have held that this inspiration is *verbal,* or, in other words, that not only were the writers of the Bible so inspired by the Holy Ghost that the *truths* which they wrote or spoke were entirely free from all admixture of error, but that the *very words* in which these truths are uttered were also inspired. This harmonizes entirely with the position which I have here assumed. The objectors to this say that, if this is so, then we should have precisely the same style, the same forms of expression, the same narratives, and the same statements of the same facts. All, however, will agree that the doctrine, the narrative, the fact is *truly* stated—so stated that there is not only perfect harmony among the inspired writers, but an infallible presentation of the truth of God. Of this there can be no doubt in the mind of any one who believes at all in the inspiration of the Sacred Scriptures. But those who make the objection referred to seem to

* Alford. Prolegomena, vol. i, p. 21.

overlook the fact that in God's word, as well as in God's works, there is perfect harmony amid great diversity. The Spirit of the Lord has taken the minds of men as they were, with all their peculiarities, their weaknesses, their limitations of knowledge, and their surroundings of country, clime, language, manners, and customs, and has put his own words into their mouths or into their minds, and has spoken through them in view of all these circumstances, and yet so that nothing written or uttered by them is, or can be, untrue. The ten commandments, or words written by God upon the tables of stone, are directly and distinctly his own words. How constantly Moses told the children of Israel that what he communicated to them from God was exactly as God commanded him! How careful he was to impress upon their minds that he was not to add unto those words, or diminish from them, under severest penalties. (Deut. iv, 2.) To quote all the places where this language is employed would be to transcribe a large part of the Pentateuch. So true is this, in fact, that if the words in which Moses spake to the people were not the words of God, he is plainly liable to the charge of gross imposture. The verbal inspiration of David's Psalms is witnessed to by Christ and his apostles: "For David himself said by the Holy Ghost, The Lord said to my Lord." Mark xii, 36. "Men and brethren, this scripture must needs have been fulfilled, which the Holy Ghost by *the mouth of David* spake." Acts i, 16. "Wherefore, as the Holy Ghost saith, To-day if ye will hear," etc. (Psa. xcv, 7.) Heb. iii, 7. Isaiah opens his sublime prophecies by calling upon the heavens and the earth to hear, for the Lord hath spoken. (Isa. i, 2.) When Jeremiah hesitated to obey the divine command, saying, "Ah, Lord God! behold, I cannot speak: for I am a child." "Then the Lord put forth his hand, and touched my mouth. And the Lord said unto me, Behold, I have put *my words* in thy mouth." Jer. i, 6, 9. Over and over again God charged Ezekiel, saying, "Thou shalt hear the word from my mouth, and shalt warn the people from me." And in almost every chapter he directly attributes all he says to the "word of the Lord which came to him."

It is needless to quote further from the Old Testament scriptures, as all the writers acknowledge directly and indirectly the same thing. And what the writers of the Old Testament declare of themselves, the writers of the New Testament accord to them. "God, who at sundry times and in divers manners spake in time past unto the fathers by the prophets." Heb. i, 1. "Holy men of God spake as they were moved by the Holy Ghost." 2 Pet. i, 21. The same verbal inspiration is claimed by the apostles. "Which things also we speak, not in the *words* which man's wisdom teacheth, but which *the Holy Ghost teacheth.*" These scriptures, I think, sufficiently prove the position which I have taken. And I may add that all those objections which Rationalists and others urge against the position, derived from the language of St. Paul in his first Epistle to the Corinthians, in the sixth and seventh chapters, and also from his directions to Timothy to bring his "cloak which he left at Troas with Carpus, and his books and parchments," may be urged with equal strength against the plenary inspiration of the apostle. The answers to these have been so frequently given that I need not attempt a reply here. I will only add the language of one of the most forcible writers of the present day, who, at the close of three articles on this subject, says, "May all Christian scholarship accept the decision of modern philology, of the laws of language, of the sanctified instincts of the faithful, of the historic Church, of the Scriptures themselves, and, with the angel of the Apocalypse, ever declare that 'these are the true *words* of God!'"*

* Rev. G. Haven, Methodist Quarterly Review, on Divine Element in Inspiration, Jan., April, July, 1868.

CHAPTER VII.

THE COMFORTER CONVINCING THE WORLD OF SIN — THE SPIRIT OF BONDAGE.

ONE of the most important announcements made by Christ as to the coming of the Comforter was this: "And when He is come, he will reprove [or convince] the world of sin, and of righteousness, and of judgment. Of sin, because they believe not on me: of righteousness, because I go to my Father, and ye see me no more; of judgment, because the prince of this world is judged." John xvi, 8–11. This announcement is important, because of the *extent* of the operations of the Comforter. "He shall reprove [convince] *the world.*" It is also important if the character of his operations is carefully regarded. He shall convince the world "of sin, of righteousness, and of judgment." The word ἐλὲγχεὶν, which our translators render "reprove," has a much deeper meaning. "It is better rendered *convince;* but still this does not express the double sense which is manifestly here intended, of a *convincing* unto salvation, and a *convicting* unto condemnation ; 're-prove' is far too weak, conveying merely the idea of an objective rebuke ; whereas the original word reaches into the heart, and works subjectively in both the above-mentioned ways."* It was not necessary that the Comforter should come to reprove the world of sin. "The words of men, the thoughts of men, the eloquence of men, would have been sufficient to do this. Every body who in any age has lived a holy life, or in any way been better than his neighbors, has done this. Even an unholy man may reprove sin. Poetry, in comedy and satire, had reproved the world of sin. Philosophy had reproved the world of sin, and its reproofs were severer and more clamorous, but vainer than ever, when the Spirit of God began his great work."† But the Comforter came to *convince* the world of sin, and in doing this he struck at the very root of all sin, namely, unbelief. "Of sin, because they believe not in me." This, indeed, is the great condemning sin of the world. In view of the great provisions of the Gospel, no

* *Vide* Alford, *in loco.*

† Hare, Mission of the Comforter, pp. 62, 63.

man is condemned solely for being a sinner, or even for being a great sinner ; but because of his not believingly accepting Christ as his Saviour. So, upon the other hand, no man is saved by his virtue, honesty, good works, holy life. He must believe in Christ, or he will come under the condemnation of the Spirit. The plan of God for making men good, pure, and holy, differs from all the ways and means of man's devising. Men see that sin exists in themselves and others. Not only so, they reprove sin ; they despise, they hate it ; they even loathe themselves on account of it. But how do they go about to remedy it ? All their efforts are merely directed against the *symptoms* of the disease. If they can only succeed in allaying or in mitigating these they rest content. But have they succeeded in even doing this ? Still, after all their efforts, the fever rages with unchecked severity—still the inflammation spreads —still death is hovering near. Or, they have tried to purify the streams of corruption ever issuing from the corrupt fountain of the human heart. They have cast into them one remedy after another, but still they have remained corrupt. Then they have vainly tried to dry up those streams. And every expedient which the human mind could conceive has been employed to this end. But still the streams flow on as from an exhaustless fountain. Failing to purify or to dry up these streams, the effort has been made to dam them up—to hold them within certain limits, or to restrict them within fixed boundaries. To this end the whole jurisprudence of the world has been directed. Codes of law have been multiplied without number. Statutes have been enacted to cover every possible case of human sin and guilt; and all of the dreadful majesty of the law-makers, of judges, and executioners, of pains and penalties, of fines and imprisonments, and even of the death-penalty, executed ofttimes with the most horrid barbarities; and yet, while many have been restrained from the outward and overt act of which alone the law can take cognizance, multitudes have still gone on in the ways of wickedness. The pent-up streams have burst forth, breaking down the barriers which had restrained them, and spreading every-where, in their fearful sweep, ruin and desolation. Or, they have endeavored to make good fruit grow upon a corrupt tree; to make grapes grow upon the thorn-bush, or figs upon the thistle. Such have been the weary and unsuccessful efforts of the world during the by-gone centuries. Nor have men yet abandoned the vain attempt. Still men look upon sin as an accident, as a misfortune, as the result of unfavorable surroundings—of birth, food, climate, or education, and they are plying their remedies accordingly.

But not so works the Comforter. He strikes at the very root and seat of the disease at once. He comes to cleanse the fountain, that its streams may be both pure and sweet; he comes to make the tree good, that its branches may be laden with ripe and luscious fruits. To save the world from sin he strikes at the very source of all sin—unbelief. Now the work of the Comforter in the heart of the unregenerate man, first of all, is to convince him of *his need of Christ.* That man has not believed that he is in need of such a Saviour is evident. He has not believed that his condition is so fearful, so perilous, and so alarming as to make it necessary for him to come to Christ. As a consequence of this he has made no effort to secure an interest in the blood of the Lamb of God, and hence has remained with all the weight of his unpardoned sins upon his soul, and with the terrible vengeance of God overhanging his unsheltered head. But when the Comforter comes to that one, he so reveals his condition to him that he sees, he *feels*, his lost and undone state, and hence he is made deeply conscious of his need of Christ—of an all-sufficient, almighty, divine Christ. And in all the long catalogue of his sins now unrolled before his eyes he sees none so dark, so aggravated, and so condemning, as that of his willful rejection of Jesus Christ. Now the Comforter becomes to him "the Spirit of bondage unto fear." He beholds himself held in a bondage the most abject, and bowed under a burden too intolerable to be borne; hence he cries out, "O wretched man that I am! Who shall deliver me from the body of this death?" Or, like Bunyan's Pilgrim, he is bound under a burden which presses him to the earth, and he seeks and sighs for deliverance. At once he is also convinced "of righteousness." Not of his own, for he has none. All his boasted "righteousnesses" now seem to him only as "filthy rags." What he wants, what he is convinced he must have, is a spotless righteousness in which to appear before God. That righteousness he sees he cannot work out for himself. He has labored at the loom for many a year for this purpose, but the garment, whatever it may be, which he has wrought out is not *the* garment which a holy God requires. The Comforter now presents Christ before him as "The Lord, our righteousness." He shows to him how he demonstrated his own righteousness by going to the Father; how, while the world crucified him as a malefactor, God the Father has honored and declared him to be his Son with power by the resurrection from the dead, and had "exalted him to his own right hand, far above all principality, and power, and every name that is named." There is also now revealed to him the way, the plan, of God's righteousness through the atoning sacrifice of Calvary, and that it is only through the blood and righteousness of Christ that it is possible for him to be constituted righteous in the sight of a holy God. And further, the *means* by which this righteousness may be obtained are made to appear. That it is not by *doing* this or that, but by *believing* on the Lord Jesus Christ that the dying sinner comes into the possession of this blood-purchased righteousness. "The righteousness which is of faith speaketh on this wise, Say not in thine heart, Who shall ascend into heaven? that is, to bring Christ down from above: or, Who shall descend into the deep? that is, to bring up Christ again from the dead. But what saith it? The word is nigh thee, even in thy mouth, and in thy heart: that is, the word of faith, which we preach; that if thou shalt confess with thy mouth the Lord Jesus, and shalt believe in thine heart that God hath raised him from the dead, thou shalt be saved." Rom. x, 6–9.

Another part of the work of the Comforter is to convince the world of "judgment"—"of judgment, because the prince of this world is judged." This does not refer primarily to the final judgment, as is generally supposed. This is a judgment which is daily and hourly being rendered. It is the conviction which the Spirit of God produces in the human soul that the judgment of this world of God's character, of Christ's atoning sacrifice, of sin and its deserved punishment, of righteousness and its absolute necessity, is all wrong, is diametrically opposed to God's judgment, and is condemned both by his divine law and the economy of his grace. This judgment of an ungodly world is formed and exercised under the power and influence of the Prince of Darkness. It is he who "blinded the minds of them which believe not, lest the light of the glorious Gospel of Christ, who is the image of God, should shine unto them." 2 Cor. iv, 4. They are not always conscious of this power which is exercised upon them ; ay, even in many instances they deny its existence ; but the Comforter will convince them of the fearful delusion under which they have been laboring, and of the awful bondage in which they have been held. For instance, under the influence of "the prince of this world" they have regarded sin as a trifling thing ; they have looked upon the service of God as a gloomy and miserable drudgery ; they have laughed at God's threatened judgments, and trifled with the terrors of his law ; they have imagined that they could live in sin and die in sin, and yet obtain at last everlasting life. Thus they have been shut up in unbelief, and thus, too, they are prejudged and precondemned. For "he that believeth not *is condemned already*, because he hath not believed in the name of the only begotten Son of God." John iii, 18. And so the Prince of this World is judged and condemned already, in premonition of his final and everlasting condemnation at the second coming of our Lord Jesus Christ. Then he shall go out no more to deceive the nations. Then he shall be "cast into the lake of fire," and "be tormented day and night for ever and ever." Rev. xx, 10.

But let it be remembered by every one that what the Comforter does in the human soul is to convince it of these things. It is not promised that he shall produce great *feeling* or deep emotion, but simply *convince* of sin, of righteousness, and of judgment. This conviction is frequently accompanied by these deep emotions, and sometimes they are alarming and overwhelming. But this is not always the case. All that the divine economy provides for, and that is enough, is to produce in the mind such a conviction of sin as that it will feel its need of Christ so as to make application to him for salvation, and believe upon him for its reception and enjoyment. Some persons who are truly convinced of sin are greatly troubled because they do not feel as they think they should, or as they have seen others feel. This is a great mistake. If man is truly convinced of his sin, of his condemnation, of his need of Christ, and of his exposure to the wrath of God, this is all that is necessary to produce in him a most earnest desire for salvation, and to call forth from him the most determined and persevering efforts for its enjoyment.

By the influence of the Comforter every human soul, in every place and age of the world, has been made conscious of sin to a greater or less extent, and with more or less clearness. It is in view of this that sacrifices have bled all along the ages, and among all nations, and men have undertaken pilgrimages, practiced penances, lacerated their bodies, tortured their limbs, and even devoted their offspring or themselves to death, to be rid of this conscious burden. The Prophet Micah gathers up into one piercing wail the universal outcry of a sin-burdened humanity in its desire to be delivered from sin and its fearful condemnation. "Wherewith shall I come before the Lord, and bow myself before the high God? shall I come before him with burnt-offerings, with calves of a year old? Will the Lord be pleased with thousands of rams, or with ten thousands of rivers of oil? shall I give my first-born for my transgression, the fruit of my body for the sin of my soul?" Micah vi, 6, 7. This consciousness of sin and guilt often becomes a burden from which the sinner groans to be delivered. This has been realized in thousands of instances. Often, under the preaching of the word, by some providence, by the sudden awakening of the conscience, in dreams of the night, by a single word spoken by a Christian friend, or even by a little child, or by a recalling of sermons, exhortations, vows, and promises—in an instant the sins of a life-time have been made to appear before the eye of the sinner, and he has been made to confront the terrible consequences of his guilt. Then a sense of bondage to fear, of a heavy burden, has come upon the soul; then fearful promonitions of a coming vengeance are realized; then the fountain of tears is unsealed; and then the cry goes up from the burdened heart, "What must I do to be saved?"

It has been often remarked of late that conviction of sin has not seemed to be so deep or so overpowering as it was in former years. One reason among others that has been assigned for this is that the masses of those who attend upon our ministrations have been religiously trained, and are consequently familiar with the truths of the Gospel, so that they do not produce that impression which they would if those truths were new or unknown. This I regard as a very unsatisfactory answer. Is it not rather true that the pulpits of our land have failed to proclaim clearly and unhesitatingly the terrors of God's law? Have not many good ministers, men of undoubted piety, been restrained from doing this for fear of offending "ears polite?" Has there not been, is there not *now*, a practical unbelief, a practical universalism, prevalent among the ministry and membership of our Churches? Have not the thunders of Sinai been hushed, and its lightnings vailed? It is, indeed, very pleasant to speak of the melting strains of Calvary, or to dwell upon the heavenly mansions, the jasper walls, and the gates of pearl. But, historically as well as experimentally, Mount Sinai comes before Mount Calvary. The Comforter not only convinces man of the fact and the existence of sin, but also of its damning character. And when

God's ministers have uttered these truths as they are in Jesus, his divine power has always accompanied the truth, and sealed it upon human hearts and consciences. We have been cowed down by the derisive cry of the godless and unbelieving world against preaching the fiery terrors of the law, and cowardly and pusillanimously we have yielded to its demand upon us to "prophesy smooth things." We are experiencing the bitter fruits of this in an emasculated Christianity—a pale, sickly, powerless thing. Let the ministry of our land, then, and of the whole world, follow the teachings of the Comforter in his divine word, and his convictions in their hearts, and let them, "knowing the terrors of the Lord, persuade men;" and not only will many more be persuaded to become Christians, but they will also go out from our sanctuaries in greater numbers, crying out, "Men and brethren, what shall we do?"*

* On this whole subject read Hare on the Mission of the Comforter.

CHAPTER VIII.

THE COMFORTER AS THE REGENERATOR.

THE law of Regeneration, or of the new birth, is absolute in the kingdom of God. "Except a man be born again, he cannot—*οὐ δύναται*—see the kingdom of God." John iii, 5. No language could more clearly express the deep, the tremendous necessity of this work. Now if all that is meant by this work is the sprinkling of a few drops of water upon the brow, or even a submergence into "the floods of great waters," or if man, by the mere exer-ercise of his volitional powers, could accomplish what it requires or imports, then we might exclude the necessity of a divine Almighty agency. But if we carefully look at what this requirement is, we shall see that no other power can accomplish it. See what is required. A man "must be born again," literally born from above —from heaven—from God. This is further expressed by the Saviour in verse 5, when he says, "Except a man be born of water and of the

Spirit"—of water as the outward and visible sign, and of the Spirit, as the divine, efficient agent— "he cannot enter into the kingdom of God."

We shall be readily convinced of the greatness of this work, and of the necessity of a divine agent for its performance, if we look carefully at the language which the word of God employs in describing it. It is called a "*quickening*." Eph. ii, 1. A being made alive from the dead. It is called a *translation* from the kingdom of darkness into the kingdom of God's dear Son. (Col. i, 13.) It is called a *new creation*, in which old things have passed away, and all things have become new. (2 Cor. v, 17.) It is frequently spoken of as a change from sin to holiness, from bondage to liberty, from darkness to light, and from death to life. Now, a work so great and so momentous as this is certainly beyond the power of men or angels to perform. Hence the word of God uniformly ascribes this work to the Spirit. (John iii, 5; Tit. iii, 5.) In other places it is ascribed to the Father, and in others still to the Son. But nowhere in the word of God is this work ascribed to man, or declared to be within his power to do.

Nowhere is it even hinted at that it can be done by baptism alone.

When we bring our children to the altars of our churches to receive the baptismal dew upon their brows, it is not that any change can be effected in their character by this act. But it is to acknowledge that our offspring inherit the rich benefits of the redemptional work of Christ, and that they are, and of right ought to be, the children of God. Baptism does not make or constitute our children children of God. They are already the children of God in Christ Jesus before baptism. And while it is the duty of parents to recognize these existing relations by this solemn and impressive rite, yet the condition and relation of the child toward God and heaven are just the same before baptism as after it. The child, subsequent to baptism, doubtless sustains a different relation to the visible Church, and the parents have acknowledged the obligations which rest upon them to give him a religious training; but otherwise no change whatever is produced. If children and adults can be saved, or regenerated, by the baptism of water alone, and if without regeneration they cannot enter into the kingdom of God, but must forever perish, then the theory and practice of compulsory baptism, as held by the Romish Church, have great show of reason and humanity in it.

But this work none but God can perform. "If," says a most earnest writer,* "it were only a little mending, a little patching, a little turning over of a new leaf, then man might do this." But when it is a *creation*, a *translation*, a *transformation*, a *resurrection*, *God must do it.* The cause must always be adequate to the production of the effect. And where, I ask, has this moral, this spiritual transformation ever occurred without the direct almighty agency of the Eternal Spirit? But by his power, countless multitudes have been thus regenerated and transformed. The instances are too numerous, indeed, to allow any more than a reference to them. They have been occurring all through the ages; and, blessed be God! they are now daily occurring. The character of the work wrought in many, very many instances, as to its reality and genuineness and blessed results, cannot be doubted by any honest mind. The work wrought has been evidently not the work of man, but of

* Ryle.

God. Truly has Mr. Wesley said, "Nothing but that power which made a world can make a Christian." Indeed, this work is only paralleled by the work of creation. "If any man be in Christ, he is a new creature"—a new creation. 2 Cor. v, 17. "God, who commanded the light to shine out of darkness, hath shined in our hearts." 2 Cor. iv, 6. What wonders has the Comforter wrought in the regeneration of human souls! Men who have been guilty of nearly every sin—bold blasphemers, relentless persecutors, licentious, covetous, extortioners, men sunken to the lowest depths of degradation and infamy—have been renewed, purified, and saved; have lived and died in the enjoyment of God's favor; and have exemplified in life and death the sweetness, the purity, and the power of saving grace. It was so in the early history of the Church; it is so now. Look at the members of the Corinthian Church. After the apostle had enumerated nearly every crime in the catalogue, he says: "And such were some of you: but ye are washed, but ye are sanctified, but ye are justified in the name of the Lord Jesus, and by the Spirit of our God." 1 Cor. vi, 11. So with the members of the Ephesian

Church; they had "walked according to the course of this world, according to the prince of the power of the air." Eph. ii, 2. They had been "dead in trespasses and in sin;" they were "children of wrath even as others." But they had been "quickened," "raised up, and made to sit together in heavenly places"—literally, in the heavenlies—"in Christ Jesus;" they were "made nigh by the blood of Christ," and "built upon the foundation of the apostles and prophets," and were growing up "unto a holy temple in the Lord." Eph. ii, 6, 13, 20, 22. The same thing was true of the Church at Colosse. Its members had been guilty of "fornication, uncleanness, inordinate affection, evil concupiscence." Col. iii, 5. But in their new state the apostle writes to them: "And you, being dead in your sins and the uncircumcision of your flesh, hath he quickened together with him, having forgiven you all trespasses; blotting out the handwriting of ordinances that was against us, which was contrary to us, and took it out of the way, nailing it to his cross." Col. ii, 13, 14. They were now "risen with Christ;" they had "put on the new man," and were "the elect of God, holy and beloved." Col. iii, 1, iii, 1, 10, 12. The Thessalonians had been worshipers of "dumb idols," and had practiced the abominable rites of that worship; but they had been turned from them "to serve the living and the true God." 1 Thess. i, 9. Their piety was eminent. They "were ensamples to all that believed in Macedonia and Achaia." Their "faith," also, "grew exceedingly, and the charity of every one of (them) you all toward each other aboundeth." 2 Thess. i, 3. And these miracles of grace have been repeated all along the ages. It is no argument against these statements that many who have professed to be Christians are not what they ought to be, and furnish no evidence whatever of any change in their character and life. All this is readily admitted; and yet the fact remains undisputed that there *are* many who, although their previous course was one of sin and shame, are now living blameless and harmless, in all the various conditions and relations of life. Now what has effected this change? Certainly it is not philosophy—it is not the adoption of any mere system of ethics—it is not the result of the self-determining power of the will—it is not a development—for that would only have been from bad to worse; it is not any condition of the natural. We must therefore conclude when such cases occur, as, blessed be God! they frequently do, that this is the work of God—that it is the result of the mighty operation of the Holy Ghost.

CHAPTER IX.

THE COMFORTER AS THE WITNESS-BEARER.

THERE are two great possibilities in the condition of every adult human being, resulting directly from the redemptional work of the Son of God. The first is, that he may be *certainly saved;* and the second is, that he may have a *certain knowledge* that he is saved. Of the first-named of these possibilities there can be no doubt in the mind of any one who believes in the sacrificial character of the death of Christ, and in the universality of the provisions of the atonement. "Christ Jesus came into the world to save sinners," (1 Tim. i, 15,) and "by the grace of God he tasted death for every man," (Heb. ii, 9,) is the grand evangel proclaimed to our world. And along with that announcement comes the blessed assurance that he that believeth on him *shall be saved,* no matter *who,* or *where,* or *what* he is. But when we come to inquire, May a man know that he is saved, that his sins are forgiven him, and that he is a child of God? many doubt, hesitate, and even deny that he may. Now, in addition to the positive evidence which I shall adduce from the word of God to sustain the position which I have assumed, there are some presumptive evidences to which the attention of the reader is desired.

It is hardly probable then, I say, that, after God has made such a provision for the salvation of the sinner at an infinite expense, when he has complied with the conditions upon which he has proffered that salvation to him, he will leave him still in doubt and uncertainty as to whether he *is* saved or not. There cannot certainly be any reason advanced why God should will that his creatures must be left in the dark upon a question of such vital importance to them. If it is his will that man should be saved—and who can doubt this?—it does seem clear that he should also will that he should know he is saved. Again, here I am, an immortal being, hurrying on through time to meet the changeless destinies of eternity, knowing that I must dwell forever either with the angels and with God, or with devils and damned spirits, and is it possible that I cannot know whither I am going? what is my actual character and relation to God and eternity? Must I live in the dark and die in the dark? Must I go on to eternity without knowing whether I shall be among the saved or the lost? Am I not to know until after probation is ended, or until the judgment is set, whether my portion shall be among the blessed or the damned? In view of these considerations I ask, Is it not presumable that if I comply with the conditions of the Gospel, and God for Christ's sake pardons my sins, he will give me a knowledge of the fact in some way?

Again, the character of the work wrought by the Holy Spirit in the soul is such that it seems probable that he would give his testimony to the fact that such a work has been done. That it *is possible* for the Comforter to do this work, or bear this witness in the soul, is evident. No person can reasonably doubt this. If he can act directly upon the mind and heart of man in producing conviction for sin, and the sense "of bondage unto fear," then he can act directly upon his mind or spirit, giving the consciousness of sins forgiven and of adoption into the divine family. This brings us at once to the question, Will he do this work? Will he bear his testimony within the heart of the actually forgiven, justified, and adopted believer, that this great change in his condition and relation has been wrought? The evidence for the affirmative of this question is clear and conclusive. The language of the apostle on this point is explicit. Writing to the Romans, he says, "Ye have not received the spirit of bondage again to fear; but ye have received the Spirit of adoption, whereby we cry, Abba, Father. The Spirit itself *beareth witness with our spirit,* that we are the children of God." Rom. viii, 15, 16. Again, "Because ye are sons, God hath sent forth the Spirit of his Son into your hearts, crying, Abba, Father." Gal. iv, 6. Hence it appears that the facts of man's pardon and adoption are not left to mere guess-work, to conjecture, to inference, or induction, but are directly revealed unto the soul by the Holy Ghost sent down from heaven. And, in fact, in no other way can this be fully or satisfactorily known. What I want to know is, Are my sins forgiven me? Of course, no one who reads this book will for a moment believe that any man or any hierarchy has the right or the power to absolve me. It is God against whom I have sinned. It is God's forgiveness that I must have. But the question still returns, "How am I to know that God has forgiven me?" "How is the act of pardon which passes in the depths of the Divine Mind to be made known to me?" The priest, assuming to stand in the place of God, may say to me, "*Absolvo te.*" But how does he know that *God* absolves me. "May he not be mistaken?" "As he is nothing but an erring man, may he not hastily and unwarrantably pronounce me forgiven when really I am not forgiven, and so, after all his absolution, may I not still be under the wrath of God?" But there are those who will tell me that I must judge from my feelings, my state and condition, whether I am a child of God or not. But this would certainly be a most unsafe ground upon which to base my hopes. I am naturally inclined to put the most favorable construction upon my character and conduct, and so I may easily deceive myself. What I want is a knowledge of this fact so clear, direct, and positive, that I need have no further doubt that this work has been wrought. But there are others still who will tell me, "You must take the word of God and compare your character, conduct, and experiences with its teachings, and if there is a correspondence, a harmony, between the written word and your experience, then you may properly and safely conclude that you are a child of God. Now this I know is all well enough in its place. This is the witness of my own spirit; but what I want is God's witness or testimony. There is nothing in the Bible which tells me that *my* "sins are forgiven me." That blessed book gives me certain marks or signs by which I may judge whether I have the general characteristics of a child of God. But I must *be* a child of God before I can have these marks. Now can I know at the time when I become a child of God that I am indeed in this blessed relation? I regard, then, the language already quoted as distinctly teaching that God has made a provision entirely adequate to meet this felt want of my soul, and the blessed Comforter is the only one in the universe who can act in this great work.

When the Son of God was upon the earth he proclaimed directly to the forgiven one, "Thy sins are forgiven thee." Matt. ix, 7; Mark ii, 5;

Luke vii, 48. But he is no longer here. He is gone away into the heavens, and "is seated at the right hand of God." But before he went he promised another Comforter to carry on his great designs and to complete his wonderful work. Now it is this Comforter which brings and bears this witness to the consciousness of the believer of his forgiveness and of his sonship. I have already referred to his eminent fitness for this work. This the apostle distinctly presents before us when he says, "What man knoweth the things of a man, save the spirit of man which is in him? even so the things of God knoweth no man, but the Spirit of God." And the Spirit of God "searcheth all things, yea, the deep things of God." 1 Cor. ii, 10, 11. Consequently, when the act of pardon passes in the Divine Mind, the Eternal Spirit is in agreement therewith, and is fully cognizant thereof. Now, then, God the Father, who, for the sake of his only-begotten Son, hath forgiven the sinner, and adopted him into his divine family, "sends forth the Spirit of his Son into the heart of the forgiven and adopted one, crying 'Abba, Father.'" That is, by his presence in the soul, and the witness which he bears to the soul, he calls forth the filial cry from the adopted child.

Does any one ask me now, "*How* is this witness borne in the soul of the believer?" I answer, I cannot fully tell, any more than I can explain the manner in which the Spirit regenerates the human soul. The manner is unknown, but the blessed fact is clear to the consciousness of the child of God. But what then is this witness? No uninspired writer ever so clearly expressed this as Mr. Wesley has done in his sermon upon this subject. He says, "By the testimony of the Spirit, I mean an inward impression on the soul, whereby the Spirit of God immediately and directly witnesses to my spirit that I am a child of God; that Jesus Christ hath loved me, and given himself for me: that all my sins are blotted out, and I, even I, am reconciled to God."* But is it not possible to be deceived about this witness? May not a person think that he has such a witness, when indeed he has it not? I answer, There is no necessity whatever for deception here, nor scarcely a possibility of it to an honest and sincere soul. For, where this witness of the Spirit is made directly to the

* Wesley's Sermons, vol. i, p. 94.

soul, there is always the corroborating testimony of our own spirit. On this point Dr. Chalmers well says, "The part which our own spirit has is, that with the eye of consciousness we read what is in ourselves, and with the eye of the understanding we read what is in the book of God's testimony. And upon our perceiving that such as the marks of grace which we find to be within so are the marks of grace which we observe in the description of that word without that the Spirit incited, we arrive at the conclusion that we are born of God."* But when he says in the same lecture, "I could not, without making my own doctrine outstrip my own experience, vouch for any other intimation of the Spirit of God than that which he gives in the act of making the word of God clear unto you, and the state of your own heart clear unto you,"† he evidently limits the word of God by the standard of his own experience. Now that the Spirit of God does all that Dr. Chalmers says, in the heart, and on the inspired page, we fully believe. But he does *more* than this. He does not leave us to an inference; he witnesses directly in the heart. And, although in conse-

* Lecture on the Romans, p. 275. † *Ibid.*, 276.

quence of the creed of Dr. Chalmers, he, and many others of the same faith, have been hindered from enjoying this clear and blessed testimony, yet this will not weigh against the clear utterance of God's revealed truth, nor the joyful experience of countless thousands of believers. This blessed witness *in* the soul is guarded by the concurrent witness *of* the soul, and thus is distinguished from "the presumption of the natural mind, and from the delusion of the devil." The word of God has certain infallible signs by which we may know whether or not the witness in our hearts is, indeed, the work of the Spirit. Wherever the witness of the Spirit is, there are, also, "the fruits of the Spirit." It is as much a matter of my own consciousness whether I have these fruits of the Spirit or not, as it is whether I now breathe and live. And if, when I am made conscious by the indwelling and witnessing of the Comforter that I am a child of God, I have also the consciousness that I have "love, joy, peace, long-suffering, gentleness, goodness, faith, meekness and temperance," (Gal. v, 22, 23,) then without presumption, and with filial confidence, I may cry, "Abba, Father." Thus the child of God may stand upon a rock, and "rejoice in hope of the glory of God." But without this clear witness of our *childship*, we can have no clear witness of our *heirship*. "*If* children, then heirs." But I must be a child before I can be an heir. And I must know that I am a child before I can know that I am an heir. If I have doubts or misgivings upon the one point, I shall certainly have them upon the other. If I am in the dark as to my sonship, I certainly shall be in the dark as to my heirship. But if I have the Spirit's witness in my soul crying within me, Abba, Father, and the fruits of the Spirit in my heart and in my life demonstrating that I am not deceived, then "I can read my title clear" to my heavenly inheritance; then all doubts and fears evanish from my mind, and then I can say, I "know if the earthly house of this tabernacle were dissolved, I have a building of God, a house not made with hands, eternal in the heavens." 2 Cor. v, 1.

This great doctrine is not peculiar to Methodism, but it has been clearly taught by the leading minds in the Church in all periods of its history. Wherever the Gospel has been clearly and powerfully preached, this great truth has been prominently brought forward, and this blessed experience, in various degrees of clearness, has been enjoyed. Luther says, "He that hath not assurance spews faith out." Melanchthon declares that, "Assurance is the dividing line between Christianity and heathenism." Rutherford writes to a friend, "Make meikle (much) of assurance, for it keepeth your anchor fast." Bishop Andrews, in his sermon on the Holy Ghost, says,* "It is the proper effect of the blood of Christ to cleanse our consciences from dead works to serve the living God; which, if we find it doth, Christ is to come to us as he is to come; and the Spirit is come, and puts his *teste,* (witness.) And if we have his *teste,* we may go our way in peace; we have kept a right feast to him, and to the memory of his coming." Bishop Hooker, in his sermon on the Certainty of Faith, says, "The Spirit which God hath given us to assure us that we are the sons of God, to enable us to call him our Father." Also, in his sermon on Jude, "Unto you, because ye are sons, God hath sent forth the Spirit of his Son into your hearts, to the end ye might know that Christ hath built you upon a rock immova-

* Watson's Institutes, vol. ii, pp. 282, 283.

ble, that he hath registered your names in the book of life." The same truth was proclaimed by Archbishop Usher, Bishop Brownrigg, Bishop Pearson, on the creed, Dr. Isaac Barrow, and a multitude of others. Stier well remarks, "That there must ever remain uncertainty among men concerning God's forgiveness in heaven, is the Pharisaic Catholic doctrine." The dying testimony of Samuel Wesley, Sen., was, "The inward witness, the inward witness, that is the proof—the strongest proof of Christianity." Mr. Wesley, while clearly announcing this doctrine, disclaims any originality, and says, "With regard to the assurance of faith, I apprehend that the whole Christian Church in the first centuries enjoyed it. For though we have few points of doctrine explicitly taught in the small remains of the ante-Nicene fathers, yet, I think, none that carefully read Clemens Romanus, Ignatius, Polycarp, Origen, or any other of them, can doubt whether either the writer himself possessed it, or all whom he mentions, as real Christians. And I really conceive, both from the *Harmonia Confessionum,* and whatever else I have occasionally read, that all reformed

Churches in Europe did once believe, 'Every true Christian has the divine evidence of his being in favor with God.'" *

And, indeed, there can be no satisfactory Christian experience without this witness. In order to be a Christian at all my sins must be forgiven me, and I am required to be a "new creature in Christ Jesus." But how am I to know that the one has been done *for* me, and the other done *in* me, unless I have the Spirit's witness? And if the Holy Ghost is not in me as an abiding guest and gift, I can certainly lay no claim to the character or the experience of a Christian. But can he abide in me without my being conscious of his presence? And if he is in me, then will he not bear his own testimony to his own work? What is any one as a Christian without the Holy Ghost? Our religion without his presence and mighty working will be nothing but a form without power, a skeleton without the living soul, a body without the spirit, a shadow without the substance. And the history of the Church clearly shows that, wherever

* "History of the Religious Movement," etc., vol. ii, p. 415, *et seq.*

this doctrine has been ignored, and this experience has been unenjoyed, it has degenerated into a heartless formalism or into a sickening ritualism. Well, then, may the whole Church now, in an agony of desire, cry out,

"*Come, Holy Comforter,*
Thy sacred witness bear
In this glad hour!
Thou who Almighty art
Now rule in every heart,
And ne'er from us depart,
Spirit of power."

CHAPTER X.

OBJECTIONS TO THE DOCTRINE OF THE DIRECT WITNESS OF THE COMFORTER CONSIDERED.

ALL important as this doctrine is, and clearly as it seems to us the Scriptures teach it, yet there have been many objections made to it which although they have been often answered, are still entertained by many honest and sincere persons.

The first I shall notice is that made by Dr. Dwight in his sermon on the "Evidences of Regeneration." * The objection is that, while some have enjoyed this witness, or assurance, the experience is by no means a common one. He says: "I am fully persuaded that the number of these persons [who enjoy this witness] is not very great. If the Christians and ministers with whom I have had opportunity to converse, many of whom have been eminently exemplary in their lives, may be allowed to stand as representatives of Christians in general, it must certainly be

* Vol. iii, p. 42.

true that the faith of assurance is not common." But to this I would reply, There can certainly be no reason, so far as the divine provision and the divine promise are concerned, why one Christian should have this witness and not another. All are certainly equally interested in knowing whether or not their sins are forgiven them—whether they are the children of God or not. There is certainly no difference in the provision made or in the promise given. The fact that the Christians and ministers referred to *did not* enjoy this grace, is no evidence whatever that they *might not* have enjoyed it. If they had specifically sought it and believed for it, would not they have enjoyed it as well as others? Certainly, or else God is a respecter of persons. The Bible gives no intimation whatever of any such favoritism in the family of God. I will readily admit that many who profess to be Christians have not this witness, and that some have it much more clearly than others. But I repeat that the fact they do not have this assurance is no argument whatever that they may not have it They are resting short of their birthright and blood-bought privileges because their faith neither perceives nor grasps those privileges. And others have this witness dimly and occasionally, simply because their faith is weak, irregular, and staggering. Thus, while those who are strong in faith cry, "Abba, Father," with an "unfaltering tongue," others lisp it with a faltering one.

The New Testament gives us clearly to understand that this was the common privilege and experience of the Christians of the first century. The apostle, writing to the Church at Rome, says: "*Ye have received* the Spirit of adoption, whereby we cry, Abba, Father. The Spirit itself beareth witness with our Spirit that we are the children of God." Rom. viii, 15, 16. So he writes to the Corinthians: "But ye are washed, but ye are sanctified, but ye are justified in the name of the Lord Jesus, and by the Spirit of our God." 1 Cor. vi, 11. And they certainly must have *known* it. Also, "For we *know* that, if our earthly house of this tabernacle were dissolved," etc. 2 Cor. v, 1. To the Galatians he writes, "Because ye are sons, God hath sent forth the Spirit of his Son into your hearts, crying, Abba, Father." Gal. iv, 6. To the Ephesians he writes, "In whom also, after that ye believed, ye were sealed with that Holy Spirit of promise, which is the earnest of our inheritance." Eph. i, 13, 14; also, ii, 1–7. He writes to the Colossians, "Who *hath* delivered us from the power of darkness, and hath translated us into the kingdom of his dear Son: in whom we *have* redemption through his blood, even the forgiveness of sins," etc. Col. i, 13–22. He says to the Thessalonians, "Our Gospel came not into you in word only, but also in power, and in the Holy Ghost, and in much assurance." 1 Thess. i, 5. "God hath also given unto us his Holy Spirit." 2 Thess. ii, 13, 14. Writing to Titus he says, "According to his mercy he saved us, by the washing of regeneration, and renewing of the Holy Ghost; which he shed on us abundantly through Jesus Christ our Saviour; that being justified by his grace, we should be made heirs according to the hope of eternal life." Titus iii, 4–7. Peter, writing to "the strangers scattered" abroad, says, "Blessed be the God and Father of our Lord Jesus Christ, which according to his abundant mercy *hath* begotten us again unto a lively hope by the resurrection of Jesus Christ from the dead." 1 Pet. i, 3. The Epistles of the beloved John are so full of this truth that nearly the whole of them would have to be quoted to notice them all; but read the following: 1 John i, 6, 7, 9; iii, 1, 2, 14; iv, 16, 17, etc. If then the early Christians did not have this witness, this assurance, the letters of the apostles to them must have been an "unintelligible jargon," and they must seriously have asked one another, "What does the apostle mean?" "We know nothing of what he writes to us." But not so; what he wrote them was the conscious and joyous experience of their souls.

Dr. Dwight in his Theology admits that "the apostles were evangelically assured of their own piety;" also, that the "first martyrs were the subjects of the same faith;" and that there are, in every country and in every age where Christianity prevails, some persons who enjoy the faith or hope of assurance." * But I think it has been clearly shown that if the apostles had this assurance, then the Christians to whom they wrote must have had it also. Almost always when speaking of this they join themselves with the body of believers. "The Spirit beareth witness with *our* Spirit," etc. "*We* know that if *our* earthly house of this tabernacle were dissolved, *we* have a building of God," etc. "*We*

* Dwight's Theology, vol. iii, pp. 41, 42.

know that *we* have passed from death unto life." And if it is true that *some* persons in every age enjoy this assurance, why may not *all* Christians enjoy it? It is objected, again, "That some persons who have professed to enjoy this witness have subsequently backslidden in heart and in life, and thus have brought disgrace upon the cause of Christ." The fact is admitted. But it does not at all affect the truth of the doctrine. Indeed, if the objection proves any thing it proves too much. For these persons, while professing to have this witness, or assurance, professed also to be Christians. Now, then, if their falling into sin proves that the doctrine of the witness of the Spirit is false, it proves likewise that the Christian religion is false. I am aware that those who hold to the Westminster Confession of Faith have difficulty in reconciling this doctrine of assurance with that of the unconditional perseverance of the saints. It is well known that their idea of assurance amounts to this, that the man who has it is not only assured of his present, but also of his eternal salvation. Now to have this knowledge, it is feared, would lead to carelessness and indifference, and even slothfulness, on the part of Christians. Therefore, in order that they may be kept watchful and diligent and prayerful, it is necessary that this question shall be kept in doubt and uncertainty. But there is also a difficulty on the other side. If a man may not, *cannot*, know that his sins are forgiven him, how can he know that he is one of God's elect? How can he know but that he may ultimately be damned? Very different from this is the Wesleyan doctrine of "the witness of the Spirit." That teaches us that the believer in Jesus may and does know that his sins are now forgiven and that he is now a child of God. But it gives him no assurance of his final and unconditional salvation. On the contrary, he is taught that this witness is only to be retained by diligently keeping all God's commandments, and walking in the same all the days of his life; that if he is unwatchful, careless, yields to temptation and falls into sin, he will lose this divine witness, and unless he is restored by penitence and faith he will ultimately perish. Again, it is objected "that the testimony of the word of God and the witness of our own spirit are all-sufficient." But it is admitted by all that we must be *actually* forgiven, and in the relationship of children of God, before we can have the testimony of the word or the testimony of our spirit. But if this work is accomplished for us it must be through the atoning sacrifice of Christ, and by the direct agency of the Holy Spirit. If, then, the Holy Spirit is present in the soul effecting its regeneration and adoption into the family of God, will he not make that soul conscious that it *is* regenerated and adopted into the family of God? Would not this supposition be natural, even if there were no direct evidence from the word of God confirming this view of the case? This view, also, limits the testimony to that of our own spirit, whereas the word of God declares there are *two* witnesses—the Spirit of God and our own spirit. It is objected again that if we have a consciousness of faith joined with true repentance we may properly conclude that we are forgiven; in other words, "I believe; I repent; therefore I am forgiven." The conclusion is correct, provided that the premises are true. Now repentance and faith are simply the *conditions* of salvation and in no sense the *evidence* of it. They also precede the acts of pardon and adoption.

But the question will arise, "How am I to know that I have truly and acceptably repented and believed? I may think that my repentance and faith are sincere and genuine, and yet I may be deceived. But even admitting that these acts of mine have been such as God requires, how am I to know that I am pardoned? Repentance and faith are acts of which my own spirit is conscious, but the act of pardon passes in the depths of the Divine Mind. How then can I know of that act unless God in some way reveal it to me? And if I do ever know it, must it not be by a direct revelation from heaven?" If we must, then, be left to the evidence of our own spirit as to our having properly performed the conditions of salvation, we must be left to doubts and fears on the one hand, or to presumptuous professions of piety on the other. The weak, the timid, the earnest and sincere, will doubt whether they have truly repented or not, while the bold and presumptuous will rest satisfied with a very slight and superficial work. There is, finally, a "hackneyed objection," as Mr. Arthur well calls it,* namely, "That it is presumption for any one to

* Tongue of Fire, p. 186.

say that he is a child of God." To this he replies, " It is never presumption to acknowledge what you are. Had David never been taken from the sheep-cot and made king it would have been presumption in him to say that he had; but when it was the case, he was bound in gratitude to own and commemorate the mercy showed to him; so if a man has not been delivered from the dominion of sin and adopted into the family of God, for him to say that such is the case is presumption; but if he has, then not to praise his Redeemer for it would be ingratitude. Saying that it is presumption for *any one* to call himself the child of God takes it for granted that no one is, or else it is absurd."

In what beautiful and blessed contrast to all these objections stands the great and glorious Gospel truth as explained and enforced by the Wesleyan theology. Here we see that the witness of the indwelling spirit is primary, giving the deep, heartfelt consciousness to the pardoned sinner that his sins are forgiven him, and that he is a child of God. Then there naturally follows the indwelling of the Spirit, his gracious fruits confirming the inward testimony and demonstrating the blessed reality. Thus, on the one hand, he is not left to grope his way in the dark, to guess, to imagine, to infer, to tremblingly hope that he is a child of God, for as he *is* a child he knows it, and rejoices in the blessed assurance ; nor, on the other hand, is he left to presumption, fanaticism, or folly, for the testimony of his own spirit is necessary to confirm his inward impression and experience. Now he knows that his repentance and faith have been accepted for Jesus' sake, that he has been enabled to meet the required conditions upon which the blessings of pardon are suspended, and that God has set his seal of approval upon him as his child ; and if ever a doubt is injected into his mind as to the reality of this work, he can instantly satisfy himself by self-examination as to whether or not he has the "fruits of the Spirit." Hence all true believers can sing,

> "His Spirit, which he gave,
> Now dwells in us, we know ;
> The witness in ourselves we have,
> And all its fruits we show.
> Our nature's turned, our mind
> Transformed in all its powers ;
> *And both the witnesses are joined,*
> *Thy Spirit, Lord, with ours.*"—C. WESLEY.

CHAPTER XI.

THE COMFORTER AS THE SEALER OF GOD'S SAINTS, AND AS THE EARNEST IN THEIR HEARTS.

BELIEVERS not only have the witness of the Spirit as to their forgiveness and adoption, but they are also sealed by the Spirit as the peculiar treasure, as the people, of God. This work is frequently referred to in the New Testament. Hence the apostle, writing to the Ephesians, says, "In whom ye (Gentiles) also trusted, after that ye heard the word of truth, the Gospel of your salvation: in whom also, after that ye believed, ye were *sealed* with that Holy Spirit of promise, which is the *earnest* of our inheritance until the redemption of the purchased possession." Eph. i, 13, 14. Also to the Corinthians he says, "Now he which stablisheth us with you in Christ, and hath anointed us, is God; who hath also *sealed* us, and given the *earnest* of the Spirit in our hearts." 1 Cor. i, 21, 22. Again, he exhorts the Ephesians,

"Grieve not the Holy Spirit of God, whereby ye are *sealed* unto the day of redemption." Eph. iv, 30. God's people, then, are a sealed people—"sealed in their foreheads" so conspicuously that they are known of him and known of a godless world. Hence the apostle writes to Timothy, "Nevertheless the foundation of God standeth sure, having this seal, The Lord *knoweth* them that are his." 2 Tim. ii, 19.

The seal has been in use from a very remote antiquity. We read of its use far back in the patriarchal times. (Gen. xxxviii, 18.) It is the instrument by which letters and other writings are stamped and ratified as evidence of their authenticity. This instrument is used by kings, states, corporate bodies, and individuals. It is not only used upon writings, but also stamped upon articles of value, and at the present day is employed largely in commerce and trade. The design of its use is to signify that the writings are authentic, actually given by the person or corporation or state which employs it, no other person or parties having a right to use it, and thus all fraud is prevented. It is also used to confirm or ratify an agreement or covenant. Again, it is used to mark as one's own property, and to make secure that which is thus marked. The process itself is simple. The instrument with some letter or device or image is stamped upon a piece of wax, of lead, or of heated iron, or upon a wafer or mucilaged stamp, and thus the exact impress of the seal is made upon the writing or the article stamped. The whole process is beautifully applied and illustrated by Cruden.*

Now believers are said to be thus sealed by the Spirit of God, and this denotes that "they are the ascertained property of God, for this is the idea conveyed by the affixing of a seal. He has received them, he claims them, he gives his attestation to the fact that they are his. It cannot, either to themselves or to any considerate observer, be any longer doubtful among what description of persons they are to be classed, nor to whom they belong." †

This sealing is by no means an evidence of final and unconditional salvation. It marks and secures the one who is now a child of God as his property. But if the Spirit is grieved by our sins or our slothfulness, the impress of this

* Cruden's Concordance, under "Seal."

† Walton on Witness of the Spirit, p. 51.

seal may be effaced from the soul. This sealing needs to be frequently renewed, for it is by no means true that *once* sealed we are *always* sealed. It is only while the Comforter abides in the soul that the sealing is kept clear and uneffaced ; but if he depart from us, then the seal will also be removed. Thus God speaks of Coniah, the son of Jehoiakim, king of Judah, that though he "were the signet upon his right hand, yet would he pluck him thence." Jer. xxii, 24. Hence, although, as we have seen, the Ephesians were sealed, yet it was not a full nor an abiding earnest of heaven to them. It was a real earnest while they took care not to "grieve the Holy Spirit of God, whereby they were sealed." And that their first sealing did not confirm their souls long is but too evident from the Saviour's message from Patmos, charging them with having "left their first love," and threatening to remove their "candlestick out of its place" unless they repented.

These facts show the absurdity of all theories of sealing which make the seal final or indelible. His seal, like every other part of his work, has to be renewed from time to time. Like his witness, it is not abiding any longer than we keep from grieving him. The Holy Spirit soon *unseals* every one who makes a bad use of his comforts. "And in unsealing the inconsistent and slothful, he evinces as much love as when he seals most fully the diligent and devotional." *

This indwelling of the Holy Ghost in the believer, witnessing and sealing, is the earnest of his heavenly inheritance; hence, as already quoted, "Ye were sealed with that Holy Spirit of promise, which is the earnest of our inherittance." Eph. i, 13, 14. So the apostle says to the Corinthians, "Now he that hath wrought us for the self-same thing is God, who also hath given unto us the earnest of the Spirit." 2 Cor. v, 5. The sealing of the Spirit and the earnest of the Spirit are distinct from each other, and yet always co-exist. The word *earnest* is from the Hebrew, עֵרָבוֹן, and signifies a pledge-earnest, a mercantile term which the Greeks and Romans appear to have adopted from the Phenicians as the founders of commerce." † In the Greek it is *ἀῤῥαβὼν*, and in the Latin *arrabo*. Thus it appears that the word was not translated by the Greeks and Latins, but merely

* Philip, "Love of the Spirit," pp. 135-137.

† Gesenius, Hebrew Lexicon *in loco*.

transferred. This word signifies, according to Webster, "A part paid or delivered beforehand, as money or goods under a contract, as a pledge and security for the whole. Thus earnest, or earnest-money, is a first payment or deposit, giving promise or assurance of a full payment, and serving also to bind the seller to the terms of agreement." * It signifies also the first-fruits which give the promise of the harvest to come. There are two things, then, especially, which the Spirit thus furnishes to the believer: first, a *pledge* of his inheritance; and, secondly, a *foretaste* of its bliss. The Spirit's witness to our sonship gives us a title to heaven, his sealing confirms our sonship and heirship, for "if children, then heirs;" and thus, long as we have the witness and the seal of the Spirit, we have the pledge of heaven. The child of God, justified and sealed, is not at once taken to heaven. He is left here to struggle against hosts of foes, to battle with adverse influences, and to travel, often a weary road, to his heavenly home. But, stranger and pilgrim though he be, unknown to, or even persecuted by, the world, often poor and despised, yet in

* Webster *in loco.*

the depths of his soul he has a title, a pledge to a mansion, a crown, a harp, a throne. He is not in heaven, but he has the pledge of heaven in his soul. That pledge is given to him, and the inheritance is sure upon one simple condition: "Be thou *faithful unto death.*" With this condition fulfilled, or while fulfilling it, he is as sure of heaven as if he were now by the throne of God. And this was not only a pledge to the early members of the Christian Church, but it is a pledge to the whole body of believers "until the redemption of the purchased possession," until all the saints are gathered home.

But not only is this earnest of the Spirit in the soul as a *pledge,* it is there also as a *foretaste.* Just as the first-fruits were a foretaste of the harvest, and a part of the harvest, so the Spirit is a foretaste of heaven—it is "heaven begun below." It is, indced, only a small part of the inheritance, a slight foretaste, but yet it *is* a part, a prelibation of what is to come. The first-fruits of the Jewish harvest might have been carried in the hands, or in a small basket or bag, while the full harvest itself filled the largest granaries and barns; so a few dollars may secure as well as foreshadow the payment of thousands, or even of millions, and the possession of that for which they are paid. Our poor hearts here can hold but little of heaven even when filled to the utmost, but that little is sweet beyond expression. It is the joy of the glorified ; it is the joy of the angels ; more than this, it is "the joy of the Lord ;" it is "joy unspeakable and full of glory." And did we live nearer to God, how much more of this earnest might we enjoy even here ! If the film of worldliness were removed from our eyes, if the mists and shadows which envelop our spirits were only rifted, if our faith were more vigorous and clear-visioned, how would the glory break over our souls ! how would the joys divine well up in our hearts ! how thin would be the vail which separates us from that heavenly world ! We permit ourselves to be robbed of much of heaven's joys by our worldly spirit, our sloth, our indifference, and our unbelief. Well does Rutherford say in one of his letters, " I dare avouch the saints know not the length and largeness of the sweet earnest, and of the sweet green sheaves before the harvest, that might be had on this side of the water if we would only take the pains." And again,

"It is our folly to postpone all till the term-day, seeing abundance of earnest will not diminish any thing from the principal sum." *

As the first-fruits of the harvest revealed to the Jew the character and abundance of the coming harvest, so the joy in the Holy Ghost which the saint has in his heart here tells him of the full and endless joys of heaven. "That is the fullness, this is the taste." That is the ocean, this is the drop. That is the endless fruition, this is only the beginning—only the day-dawn. But O, if the drops are so sweet, what will the ocean be? O, if the taste is so ravishing, what will the fullness be? A recent writer has well said, "Heaven is only the maturer, brighter, fuller development of that state which has begun in the individual heart. Joys here are like a few flowers retaining their Eden fragrance that the spirit may long for the climes where they bloom perpetually. They are a few notes of heavenly harpers, that the soul may be led to desire to join in the eternal jubilee. They are glimpses of glory in which the soul may see those hours which, like the hours on the sun-dial, are measured only by sunshine, and

* Rutherford's Letters.

of which, through eternity, there will be no end." *

Thus the sealed believer has both the pledge and the foretaste of heaven, until he enters upon his everlasting inheritance, and partakes, at the fountain-head, of its everlasting joys.

> "I would not wait for heaven ;
> Heaven may begin below ;
> To every newborn soul 'tis given
> A present God to know."

* Cumming's "Voices of the Night," p. 50.

CHAPTER XII.

THE COMFORTER AS OUR INTERCESSOR.

"LIKEWISE the Spirit also helpeth our infirmities: for we know not what we should pray for as we ought: but the Spirit maketh intercession for us with groanings which cannot be uttered." Rom. viii, 26. The question at once arises here, "In what sense does the Comforter make intercession for us?" To this I would answer, His intercession is entirely different from that which Christ, as our great High Priest, makes for us. His intercession is based upon his own merits; the Comforter's intercession is occasioned by our weakness. Christ's intercession is before the throne; the Spirit makes intercession within our hearts. Christ intercedes for us as our Advocate; the Spirit as an enlightener and helper in our petitions. The intercession of Christ for us is unconditional; that of the Comforter is conditioned upon our willingness and desire to come to God.

1. First, then, his office is *to help us to pray.*

When man is made conscious of his sinfulness, he is at the same time made conscious of his helplessness. His first thoughts are, "I cannot pray;" "I do not know how to pray;" "How dare such a sinful worm as I am approach unto God?" With these reflections his whole soul shrinks from an interview with a holy God. Like the Publican, he stands afar off, not daring to lift up his eyes to heaven, the dwelling-place of infinite purity; but, smiting upon his agonized breast, he cries out, "God be merciful to me a sinner!"

There are also many periods in the history of the child of God when, assaulted by the powers of darkness, or overwhelmed with trials, or crushed by the bereaving stroke, or sunk into the lowest depths of humiliation by a sense of his vileness and unworthiness, he feels that he *cannot pray.* It is then that the Comforter comes in with his divine help. The timid, shrinking heart is now encouraged by his presence and his aid, and emboldened to speak out its wants, or at least to groan out its desires. Thus the worm is enabled to speak unto God, and dust and ashes talk to "the Great, the Holy, and the High."

"The word translated 'helpeth' signifies to lay hold of any thing, as of a beam or burden, together with another. In ourselves we know not what to pray for or how to pray. But the Holy Spirit of God which dwelleth in us, knowing our wants better than we, himself pleads in our prayers, raising us to higher and holier desires than we can express in words, which can only find utterance in sighs and aspirations. But although these yearnings are inexpressible in words, the Searcher of hearts recognizes in them what is the minding of the Spirit, because these inarticulate pleadings of the Holy Ghost, in and for his saints, are in perfect unison with his own mind, (*κατὰ θεὸν*;) they are God-like." *

2. The Comforter by his divine illumination makes us *conscious* of our *condition* and our *wants*, so far, at least, as we can bear to see them. We know not ourselves, our actual condition, nor the deep and alarming necessities of our being. Nor could we probably bear to see ourselves as we are seen by the eye of infinite purity. It is natural for us to put the most favorable construction upon every thing appertaining to our character and condition.

* The Spirit of Life, pp. 154, 155.

We are all inclined to lay the flattering unction to our souls that all is well; to cry "Peace! peace!" when God has not spoken peace. Nor does the true Christian always realize his condition, his privileges, and the glorious possibilities of his being. Hence the Holy Spirit shines in upon the darkness of the mind, reveals our condition, creates the sense of want, inspires the soul with earnest longings, produces "hungerings and thirstings after righteousness," and thus leads us up to God. It is in view of this that we read of Christians "praying in the Holy Ghost," of their "making supplication in the Spirit." Jude xx; Eph. vi, 19.

3. Here, then, we see the *source of those unutterable groanings* which the true penitent and the true Christian often experience. They are not natural to man. They do not arise spontaneously in the human soul. They are begotten by the Holy Ghost. They are the results of his mighty operations. They occur in great crises of our history and experience. It is in the midst of them that the soul rises up to meet God, to take hold upon his Omnipotence, to test the power of the cleansing blood of Calvary, and to enter upon the higher walks of

the Christian life. And yet, in its enlarged desires, in its crushing burden of wants, it can find no language in which to express its struggling emotions. Prostrate in the dust at the foot of the throne, the lips are dumb, the words are lost, or fail to utter what now is so deeply felt, and naught but groans and sighs escape the breast of the burdened and troubled one. So Moses groaned in spirit before God when he said, "Oh, this people have sinned a great sin, and have made them gods of gold. Yet now, if thou wilt forgive their sin—; and if not, blot me, I pray thee, out of thy book which thou hast written." Exod. xxxii, 31, 32. So Hannah prayed: "She spake in her heart; only her lips moved, but her voice was not heard," etc. 1 Sam. i, 13-16. The secret of all this was she was a "woman of a sorrowful spirit;" and "out of the abundance of her complaint and grief" she had spoken unto God. So Hezekiah prayed when his life was in danger: "Like a crane or a swallow, so did I chatter: I did mourn as a dove: mine eyes fail with looking upward: O Lord, I am oppressed; undertake for me." Isa. xxxviii, 14.

On this passage Tholuck thus speaks: "That

in those moments when the soul turns with deepest ardor to its original, it is not that which is human in man, that rises Godward, but the Divine Spirit in the human breast which seeks to meet God, the profound thinkers of every clime have been aware." He instances the following from the Methnewi of Dschelaleddin, (Cod. M.S., Bibl. Reg., Ber. T. III, p. 146,) where the writer thus sings of a Mohammedan saint:

"O never think a prayer like this like other prayer; for know,
It is not mortal man, but God, from whom the accents flow.
Behold, God prays! the lowly saint stands deep abased the while,
And God who gave the humbled mind upon his prayers will smile."

Also, on page 13 of the same work he sings:

"'Allah!' was all night long the cry of one oppressed with care,
Till softened was his heart, and sweet became his lips with prayer.
Then near the subtle tempter stole, and spake, 'Fond babbler, cease!'
For not one *Here am I* has God ere sent to give thee peace!'
With sorrow sank the suppliant's heart, and all his senses fled,
But, lo! at midnight, Chiser * came, and gently spake and said,

* Name of Elias, whom the Easterns describe as Counselor of Men.

'What ails thee now, my child, and whence art thou afraid to
pray,
And why thy former love dost thou repent? declare, and
say!'
'Ah!' cries he, 'Never once to me spoke God, *Here am I,
Son.*'
Cast off methinks I am, and warned far from his gracious
throne.'
To whom Elias, 'Hear, my son, the word from God I bear.
"Go tell," he said, "yon mourner sunk in sorrow and
despair.
Each *Lord appear*, thy lips pronounce contains my—
Here am I.
A special messenger I send beneath thine every sigh.
Thy love is but a girdle of the love I bear to thee,
And sleeping in thy *Come, O Lord*, there lies, *Here, Son*,
from me."' *

4. In such intercession there is frequently an assurance accompanying, or immediately following it, *that the prayer is heard.* The experience of God's saints, in recorded instances not a few, clearly demonstrates the truthfulness of this statement. After a period of intense longing, of unutterable groanings of soul, either for themselves, or for others, suddenly, but with fullest assurance, there is realized the faith that the prayer is heard, that the answer is granted. So when John Knox prayed, "Give me Scotland, or I die," he rose up from his knees assured

* Tholuck on Romans, pp. 269, 270.

that his prayer had prevailed with God. This is remarkably illustrated in the case of the brother of Melville Cox, the heroic Missionary to Africa.

"The following are the facts: they occurred when Mr. Cox was about twenty years of age. At the time of this singular incident his brother James, who, it will be seen, was concerned in the affair, was at sea, being master of the brig 'Charles Faucet,' which was then on her passage to New Orleans. This young gentleman, although well fitted for his business in every other respect, and irreproachable in his conduct among men, was destitute of religion.

"From the hour that James sailed for New Orleans, Melville, with another brother of his, and who was alike partner in his 'precious faith,' made the absent brother a constant subject of prayer. Such, indeed, were their feelings for James, and so absorbing to them was the great question of his soul's salvation, that it became for a few weeks with them their first and last thoughts for the day.

"One evening, just as the sun had fallen, the two brothers, as they were sometimes wont to do, visited the edge of the woods back of the village where they then resided, and there knelt down to pray. The first object of interest before them was their absent brother, whose image came up to their view with more than ordinary distinctness, and who, it seemed to them, was not only far away on the sea, tossed upon its waves as the spirit of the storm might drive him, but 'without hope, without God in the world,' and liable to fall into the gulf of woe. As they prayed, their own spirits seemed in agony for James, and they poured out their feelings in alternate offerings, with a depth of sympathy, of religious fervor, of faith in God, never before experienced by them for him. It was given to them to wrestle with God in prayer, and to importune as for their own souls. And thus they did, unconscious of the nightly dews that were falling upon them, until the conflict seemed past, and the blessing they sought gained. They both rose from prayer, and, without exchanging a word upon the subject of their feelings, went to their different homes for the night.

"The next morning the brothers met; but the feelings of the past night were yet too vivid to be dissipated. Said Melville to the younger,

'What did you think of our feelings last night?' 'I think,' said the younger brother, 'James has experienced religion.' 'Well, I think,' said Melville, 'THAT HE IS DEAD; and I have put it down in my diary, and you will see if it is not true.' A few weeks passed away, and tidings came that *James was dead!* He died within a few days' sail of the Balize, in the evening, and, as the brothers supposed, by a comparison of the letter they received with Melville's diary, *on the same hour in which they were engaged in prayer for his soul.*

"The above letter contained no reference to his religious feelings, so that the correctness of the younger brother's impressions was yet to be determined. On the return of the brig, however, it was ascertained by conversation with the mate that the feelings of both were equally true. It appeared from the mate's testimony and other circumstances, that immediately after his sailing James became *serious*, abandoned profaneness, to which he had been accustomed for years, and forbade the indulgence of this profitless and degrading crime on board his vessel, and this seriousness continued to the hour of his death. He communicated his thoughts, however, to no one, excepting to his friends, upon paper, which they received after his death. Yet it does not appear from any of these circumstances that he found peace to his mind, unless it were in his last hour.

"On the morning of the day on which he died he said to his mate he thought he should die that day, and accordingly made what arrangements he could for such an event. He gave some directions about the vessel, and requested a lock of hair to be cut from his head, which, with a ring that he took from his finger, was handed to his friends. He then gave himself up to his fate. In the evening the mate went below; and, seeing quite a change had taken place in his appearance, and that death was rapidly approaching, he took his hand and thus addressed him: 'Captain Cox, you are a very sick man.' 'Yes, I know it,' was calmly, though feebly, articulated. 'You are dying,' continued the mate. 'Yes, I know it,' he again whispered. 'And are you willing?' 'Yes, blessed' — and burst into a flood of tears and expired."

The conviction, simultaneously impressed upon the minds of these brothers, that their prayer was heard, was doubtless produced by the Holy Ghost. The impression regarding the *death* of their brother is a psychological fact, well deserving the consideration of the philosopher.

But time would fail to tell of all the instances on record ; while every earnest saint in all the ages has known the truth of this—although this fact in his experience may have been known only to himself and his God. The answer is in the prayer. The same Spirit which creates the desire and produces the groanings of soul is present with the answer. The desire has come from God—it is in accordance with the will of God ; the answer is sure.

My prayer hath power with God ; the grace
  Unspeakable I now receive ;
Through faith I see thee face to face ;
  I see thee face to face and live!
In vain I have not wept and strove ;
Thy nature and thy name is Love.—C. WESLEY.

CHAPTER XIII.

THE COMFORTER AS A LEADER AND GUIDE.

"AS many as are led by the Spirit of God, they are the sons of God." But what is it to be *led* by the Spirit of God? It will readily be seen that a right answer to this question is of the greatest importance. An error here may lead the mind very far astray, either into the vagaries of mysticism on the one hand, or the delusions of fanaticism on the other. There have been persons at various periods in the history of the Church who have imagined that they were, and declared themselves to be, under the guidance of the Spirit; and yet they have been guilty in some instances of the most fanatical conduct, and in others, of the most abominable excesses. I would inquire, then, Is it possible for us to *know* when we are led by the Spirit of God? Can his guidance be distinguished from the actings of our own minds, or the decisions and determinations of our own wills? Or, on the other hand, are all who profess to be led by the Spirit fanatics and deceivers? One thing is settled for us right here, and that is, that the sons, or children of God, *are led* by the Spirit. Then, again, the Saviour expressly promised to his disciples that the Comforter should "guide them into all truth." John xvi, 13.

But the word of God names several conditions the existence of which is essential to the enjoyment of this leading and guidance. And, first of all, it is only those who are *sons* of God who are thus led. This implies that they have repented of their sins, have believed on the Lord Jesus Christ, and have experienced his justifying and renewing grace. It involves, also, the further fact that there is a complete submission of the soul to the dictates and control of the Divine Spirit. In other words, if the Holy Spirit actually leads a man, he must be willing to be led just in the way he would have him go. It would, indeed, be a great comfort to many persons if they could convince themselves and others that the way in which they go, and the actions which they perform, are from the promptings and leadings of the Holy Ghost: if, in other words, they could practice the most gross immoralities, the most impure conduct which their base hearts or their corrupt passions incline them to, and yet throw the responsibility upon the Holy Ghost. Some have ventured so far as to do these very things. Their blasphemy is of the most fearful character, for they are ascribing the works of the devil to the Spirit of God, and thus are bringing upon themselves the terrible judgments of heaven. The word of God gives us clearly to understand that no person who performs an unholy or impure action can possibly be led to do this by the Holy Ghost. The infinite purity and holiness of his character render such a thing infinitely impossible. But, on the other hand, he can only lead a person to do that which is right and just and true and good. If any man's conduct varies from these principles, no matter what his professions or pretensions may be as to his being led by the Spirit of God, "he is a liar, and the truth is not in him." There are but two spirits in the world which lead and control men's minds—the Spirit of light and the spirit of darkness; the Spirit of truth and the spirit of error; the Spirit of God and the spirit of the devil. These are in direct and eternal antagonism. They can never coalesce, or co-exist. Satan, it is true, may appear as an "angel of light," but he is no less a devil under this garb than in his own thunder-scarred deformity. Error may put on the garb of truth, but it is error still. When, therefore, the Spirit of God leads a man, he leads him to do right, to do good, to believe the truth and embrace it. The promise is emphatic, " He shall guide you into all the truth," not into error, not into folly, not into sin.

The question may arise here, " How am I to *know* what is truth ? " " The theological world," it may be said, " is a Babel of confused opinions and theories ; science seems to be opposed to some of the teachings of the Bible, and the wisest and the best men differ widely upon some important passages of Scripture ; how, in the midst of all this confusion, am I to perceive the truth ? " Let me say right here that the Bible does not profess or aim to teach philosophy or science. It does not attempt to formulate any system of astronomy, geology, chemistry, or geognosy. But it does profess to teach man about God, his character and relations to his creatures ; about man, his origin, his character, his fall, his redemption by Christ, and his destiny. Its allusions to those questions which belong to philosophical or scientific investigation, as we have already seen, are made in the language of the existing ideas and knowledge of the people among whom its truths were primarily uttered, and are merely occasional and incidental. But upon the great questions on which it does profess to give man light and knowledge it speaks out clearly and unmistakably. "The wayfaring men, although fools, *shall* not err therein." Isa. xxxv, 8. "To us at this day this word has come, and to us at this day the anointing from the Holy One flows down. For you, for me, (thank God!) the teaching of the Spirit remains. It remains for the servants and the handmaids, and many an obscure and lowly brother in the streets around us can say for himself, as truly as St. Paul could say, 'I have received the Spirit that is of God, that I may know the things which are freely given me of God.' But one who thus speaks can know that his convictions are really the teaching of the Spirit of God only so far as they correspond with the eternal types of truth, which ascertain to us what the teaching of the Spirit is. Now, as in the apostolic days, he which is spiritual can show that he is so only 'by acknowledging that the things which' these appointed teachers 'wrote to us are commandments of the Lord;'

for the gift of the Holy Ghost to others is not a gift whereby they originate the knowledge of new truths, but a gift whereby they recognize and apprehend the old unchanging mystery, still receiving afresh the one revelation of Christ, ever approaching, never surpassing the comprehensive but immovable boundaries of the faith once delivered to the saints. This is the gift which makes the written word a living word, which fills a Church with joy, and seals a soul for glory." *

Again, The Spirit of God never leads a man to *believe* any thing contrary to the word of God, or to *do* any thing contrary to its teachings. It is right here that we have an all-sufficient check against error and fanaticism. If any person thinks or feels that he is led by the Spirit of God, he is to test his impressions by the truths of God's word. If the convictions, impressions, or inclinations of his mind and heart are in accordance with the eternal truths of that word, then he may safely follow them, and properly conclude that the Spirit of the Lord is leading and guiding him aright. But if they are not in harmony with the word, then the sooner he gets rid of

* Bernard's Progress of Doctrine in the New Testament.

them the better it will be for himself and for all concerned; for it is not the Spirit of God, but the spirit of "that wicked one" which is endeavoring to lead him astray. There are those who profess to be entirely governed by their impressions, and who ascribe all those impressions to the Holy Spirit. Such governance will commonly lead those astray who follow it. Nothing is more variable and uncertain than our feelings and impressions. We are creatures subject to a thousand influences both from within and without. Some of our impressions are healthy and right, others are morbid and wrong. Some are from a sound normal condition of our physical system, and others from its deranged and disordered conditions. Some are from the world without us, and some are from the world within us. Some are from the Spirit of God, and some are from the devil. Now, then, we are commanded not to believe every spirit, but to *try* the spirits whether they are of God. (1 John iv, 1.)

We are to try our impressions by the word of God, according to its eternal principles of truth and right. And just here comes in that right, aye, that *duty,* of private judgment in reading and endeavoring to understand the word of God.

God has given to his intelligent creatures powers of reason, of judgment, of understanding, of analysis and synthesis. These are to be brought into exercise in reading the word of God, in humble reliance upon the promised aid of the Divine Spirit. Given, then, the word of God in our hands, the Spirit of God in our hearts, and our God-given reason duly enthroned in our minds, and no man need to, or will, go far astray. But any one who relies upon mere impressions will go astray into the wildest fancies, or the grossest irregularities, or the most mortifying blunders. Some very good, although at the time very mistaking, people, have done very singular, and even very ludicrous, things in following out their mere impressions. And there can be no doubt that God has permitted them to be thus humbled in order to save them from greater errors and mistakes. The well-known instance in the life of Dr. Nathan Bangs is here in point. "At a certain time when he was laboring in Canada, when the weather was very cold and the snow deep, as he was riding along the road he came opposite a dwelling that stood quite a distance from the road in the field. Instantly he was impressed to go to the house and talk and pray with its family. He could see no path through the deep snow, and he felt reluctant to wade that distance. He resolved not to go. No sooner had he passed the house than the impression became doubly strong, and he was constrained to turn back. He fastened his horse to the fence, waded through the snow to the house, and *not a soul was there.* From that time he resolved never to confide in *mere impressions.*" *

But all this, while it guards, does not militate against the doctrine of the guidance of the Spirit as taught so clearly in the word of God. In every dispensation of God's mercy and grace toward our world this great truth has been taught, and this experience has been realized. Enoch, in his three-century walk with God; Abraham, leaving Ur of the Chaldees, and going out under the Divine guidance, not knowing whither he went, but following that guidance toward Canaan, and "the city which hath foundations." The royal Psalmist very frequently in his rapt and sublime utterances refers to this truth, and dwells upon it with holy rapture: "This God is our God for ever and ever: he will

* Life and Times of Nathan Bangs, D. D., p. 101.

be our *guide* even unto death." Psa. xlviii, 14. "The meek will he guide in judgment: and the meek will he teach his way." Psa. xxv, 9. "Thou shalt *guide* me with thy counsel, and afterward receive me to glory." Psa. lxxiii, 24. "The steps of a good man are ordered by the Lord." Psa. xxxvii, 23. "Teach me to do thy will; . . . thy Spirit is good; lead me into the land of uprightness." Psa. cxliii, 10. The apostle John, writing to his brethren, says, "But ye have an unction from the Holy One, and ye know all things." 1 John ii, 20. "But the anointing which ye have received of him abideth in you, and ye need not that any man teach you: but as the same anointing teacheth you of all things, and is truth, and is no lie, and even as it hath taught you, ye shall abide in him." 1 John ii, 27.

All these Scriptures thus clearly teach a divine leadership, a divine guidance. Yes, poor, feeble, erring man may be led by the Spirit of God into all truth and righteousness; may be led through all the wildering mazes of this world up to the gates of pearl and the fadeless mansions. And O, if we oftener sought his guidance, if our hearts were only more willing to follow where he would lead, how many errors, straits, difficulties, and troubles we might avoid, and how would we be led by the side of the still waters, up to the lofty altitudes of communion with God, down into the hallowed depths of love divine, and into the immeasurable riches of divine grace! But we so often want our own will and our own way; and when the Spirit would lead us we shrink back, or refuse to follow, because the way looks to us rough and thorny, or a cross lies directly in the path. We too seldom think that the way of the cross is the way to the crown, and that the rough and thorny path leads upward to the golden streets. If we fail to follow where the Spirit leads we are losers always—losers in every way.

I cannot, however, leave this subject without noticing that this blessed fact of a Divine Leader and Guide is not only one of the deepest interest and importance, but, also, of the greatest *satisfaction and comfort.* Full well do we know that where he leads there it is not only safe for us to follow, but it is best for us to go. Sometimes the way may be one of difficulty, sorrow, and trial. We may shrink, at first, from entering upon it. But if we will only follow where our Lord doth lead all will be well. Jesus, the divine Jesus, "was *led up of the Spirit* into the wilderness to be tempted of the devil." Matt. iv, 1. Fierce, determined, persistent were Satan's attacks; but when the struggle was over "angels came and ministered unto him." Matt. iv, 11. So will it ever be with us. In the wilderness of life the Spirit may lead us to scenes of fierce temptation, as he led our Lord; but the conflict ended, the victory ours, angel pinions will fan our heated brows, and angel hands will minister to our comfort. Again, while the Church at Antioch with its "prophets and teachers," "ministered to the Lord, and fasted, the Holy Ghost said, Separate me Barnabas and Saul for the work whereunto I have called them." Acts xiii, 2. Obedient to the Divine direction, they departed on a long journey, involving dangers and perils and persecutions innumerable. But they returned with a song of triumph in their hearts and on their lips: "Now thanks be unto God, which always causeth us to triumph in Christ, and maketh manifest the savor of his knowledge by us in every place." 2 Cor. ii, 14. These instances will suffice to show that, however difficult or dangerous the way may be in which we are led, the result will be, if we follow the Divine guidance, peace, comfort, and joy. But sometimes, O how often! he will "lead us by the still waters, and make us to lie down in the green pastures," where Eden flowers bloom and shed their fragrance all around, where the skies are bright and cloudless, and all the air is burdened with celestial melodies.

But let me say, further, however rough, or thorny, or dark, the way may be at times over which the Spirit leads us, yet if we are assured that it is his hand which is guiding our steps, we may walk on with the utmost confidence and joy. What though the billows of some Red Sea may roll darkly before our eyes, and seem to forbid our advance even when the voice of God bids us "go forward!" If we will only obey the Divine command, those dark billows will be rolled up into walls of adamant; "the depths will be congealed in the heart of the sea," and the slimy paths of the monsters of the deep will be reared into a highway, over which we shall pass to sing songs of victory on the shore that lies nearest to Canaan. Or, if we are led into a den which has quivered and shaken with the thundering roar of hungry lions eager for their prey that den will be a downy couch, prepared by angel hands after they shall have locked the lion's jaws; and through the livelong night their wings will canopy our heads, and their gleaming spear-heads will defend us from harm. Mayhap we shall be led into some seven-times heated furnace of affliction in obeying his divine command. But even then the fire-flame will become as harmless as a gilded drapery, while, inconsumable as asbestos, we walk triumphantly with our Lord in the midst of the fire. Yes, if he lead us there, even martyr-tortures, martyr-dungeons, and martyr-stakes shall be turned into scenes of rapturous triumph and joy. Thus the Comforter leadeth us to mountain-tops radiant and rosy with the light of God—to valleys of humiliation, sometimes resonant with sighs and groans, and then ringing with shouts of victory and triumph. But, blessed Comforter, only let us know that *thou* leadest us and we will follow thee!

We have, then, a sure and certain guide, whom we can always follow with the utmost confidence. Amid all the wildering mazes of our earthly course, amid all the perplexing cares of life, through all its waves of trouble and sorrow, here is a Guide who is ever near. And with the divine word in our hands, and the divine Comforter in our hearts, we not only *need not*, but, we positively *shall not*, go astray. Well may we join in the prayer of the poet as we close this chapter:

"While life's dark maze I tread,
And griefs around me spread,
Be thou my guide;
Bid darkness turn to day;
Wipe sorrow's tears away,
Nor let me ever stray
From thee aside."

THE GUIDING HAND.

"'Is this the way, my Father?' ''Tis, my child;
Thou must pass through this tangled, dreary wild
If thou would'st reach the city undefiled,
Thy peaceful home above.'

"'But enemies are round!' 'Yes, child, I know
That where thou least expect thou'lt find a foe;
But victor thou shalt prove o'er all below;
Only seek strength above.'

"'My Father, it is dark!' 'Child, take my hand;
Cling close to me; I'll lead thee through the land;
Trust my all-seeing care; so shalt thou stand
'Midst glory bright above.'

"'My footsteps seem to slide!' 'Child, only raise
Thine eye to me, then in these slippery ways
I will hold up thy goings; thou shalt praise
Me for each step, above.'

"'O, Father, I am weary!' 'Lean thy head
Upon my breast. It was my love that spread
Thy rugged path; hope on, till I have said,
"Rest, rest for aye, above."'"

CHAPTER XIV.

THE COMFORTER AS THE SANCTIFIER.

THE Holy Ghost is the Sanctifier. So the word of truth uniformly declares. "We are bound to give thanks always to God for you, brethren beloved of the Lord, because God hath from the beginning chosen you to salvation *through sanctification of the Spirit* and belief of the truth." 2 Thess. ii, 13. The Apostle Peter, writing to the "strangers scattered throughout Pontus, Galatia, Cappadocia, Asia, and Bithynia," calls them "elect according to the foreknowledge of God the Father, *through sanctification of the Spirit,* unto obedience and sprinkling of the blood of Jesus." 1 Pet. i, 1, 2. But the question arises just here, "What is that sanctification which the Spirit of God accomplishes in the soul of the believer?" The word "sanctify" has two meanings, which are correlative, the one implying, but not necessarily including, the other. One is "to set apart," "devote," "consecrate;" the other is "to hallow," or "to make holy." The word is frequently used in both of these ways in the word of God. Hence we read that the first-born of Israel were sanctified to God, that is, set apart, devoted to the Lord. (Exod. xiii, 2.) They were redeemed, and therefore set apart. So also the tabernacle, and afterward the temple, the priests, the altars, the sacrifices were sanctified, or set apart, for sacred uses and purposes. It is also used in the sense of cleansing from sin, or making holy. In the New Testament the word as applied to believers always signifies purity, holiness. "And such were some of you: but ye are washed, but ye are sanctified, but ye are justified in the name of the Lord Jesus, and by the Spirit of our God." 1 Cor. vi, 11. "Christ also loved the Church, and gave himself for it; that he might sanctify and cleanse it with the washing of water by the word." Eph. v, 25, 26. "The very God of peace sanctify you wholly; and I pray God your whole spirit and soul and body be preserved *blameless* unto the coming of our Lord Jesus Christ." 1 Thess. v, 23. "Wherefore Jesus also, that he might sanctify the people with his own blood, suffered without the gate." Heb. xiii, 12. "This is the will of God, even your sanctification, that ye should abstain from fornication." 1 Thess. iv, 3.

Among all evangelical Christians these definitions are regarded as entirely in harmony with the divine teachings, and there is no difference of opinion as to the nature of the work, about the truth and the blood by which it is accomplished, or as to the Almighty Agent who alone can perform it. The only real difference of opinion among them is as to the *time* when it may be performed, experienced, and enjoyed. This, however, I shall notice more fully hereafter.

At present let us look at the work of the Spirit in effecting this wonderful transformation and purification in the human soul.

1. The Holy Spirit convinces the believer of the *necessity* of this work. This he does in two ways: (1.) By his inward operations upon the soul, revealing to it the corruptions which remain after the work of regeneration has been performed; and, (2.) By shedding his light upon the sacred page, thus revealing the duty and the privilege of the believer unto him. The theory which to some minds appears so beautiful,

that men are *entirely* sanctified when they are justified and regenerated, is regarded by nearly the whole Christian Church as in conflict with the teachings of God's word, and contradictory to the universal experience of the Church of God. It is possible for us to conceive a person whose faith at the time of his experiencing justifying and renewing grace grasps in the whole work, and then, of course, it would be done ; and it may be also that in the progressive development of Christian doctrine, and in the increasing light which will shine upon this question, such experience will become more general ; but up to this time the instances, if such there are, are exceedingly rare. The common experience of all Christians is substantially as follows : After the first gush of the raptures of pardon, and the first clear consciousness of "the renewing of the Holy Ghost," which is prolonged sometimes for days and even weeks—there is revealed to the new-born child of God, by the Holy Spirit, that there are remaining corruptions, or sins in his heart. So clearly, indeed, is this revelation made to him that no doubt exists in his mind as to the fact. He not only *sees* them, but he also *feels* them there

They do not dominate in his soul, they do not overcome the newly implanted graces of the Spirit, but they struggle for the mastery. "The flesh lusteth against the Spirit, and the Spirit against the flesh: and these are contrary the one to the other; so that ye cannot do the things that ye would." Gal. v, 17. Anger, pride, the love of the world, of its wealth, honors, fashions, and follies; "the lust of the flesh, the lust of the eye, and the pride of life," are all consciously existent in the believer's soul, clamoring for supremacy, but controlled by grace. At first the revelation of these to the young Christian is cause of inexpressible grief. Sometimes he is led even to doubt whether he was ever made the subject of saving grace. "How can I be a child of God," he asks, "when so much of sin remains in my soul?" The discovery is truly and always a painful one. To one who has been exulting in the rapturous heights of pardon and salvation thus to be led to view his condition is cause of sorrow and humiliation; but it is thus that the Comforter would lead the soul, not to undervalue the great and wonderful work already wrought, but to seek after a higher life, a fuller conformity to

God, and the spotless purity which the blood of Jesus can impart. No one who has ever experienced the saving grace of God can understandingly place a light estimate upon it; indeed, the *most difficult* part of the work of his salvation has now been wrought. He has abandoned his sins, he has believed on the Lord Jesus Christ with a heart unto righteousness, and, as the blessed result, his sins and iniquities are remembered against him no more. He is "justified freely," he is born of the Spirit, he is adopted into the divine family, and consequently becomes "an heir of God and a joint-heir with Jesus Christ." In this blessed relation "he stands and rejoices in hope of the glory of God," and his "hope maketh him not ashamed, because the love of God is shed abroad in his heart by the Holy Ghost which is given to him." All the graces of the Spirit in regeneration are implanted in his soul, and while he is faithful to God, they are ever growing there. Now I say that no person who has ever enjoyed this state and relation can speak lightly of them. All such expressions as "only justified," "merely regenerated," should never be employed.

But the inquiry arises here, "If what has

been done already is so great and glorious, can any thing further be attained or enjoyed by the believer?" Yes, for the Comforter, in his word and in the heart, convinces the believer of the necessity and desirableness of a higher life, of a closer walk with God.

2. But not only so. He shows by the same means the *possibility of experiencing and enjoying it.* It would be to confuse and discourage the child of God, if convinced of the remains of sin in his heart, and at the same time of the command of God requiring him to "be holy," to "go on to perfection," etc., he were assured that the attainment of such a state is an utter impossibility. But, blessed be God! the Comforter who convinces of the *necessity* of this work points us also to the *possibility* of its enjoyment. Oui blessed Saviour in his intercessory prayer says, "Sanctify them through thy truth: thy word is truth." John xvii, 17. So the Holy Spirit who inspired the word brings to the mind its promises and assurances, and reveals the rich provisions of infinite love. Does the child of God groan over his impurities and corruptions? He is pointed to the fountain over which is written, "The

blood of Jesus Christ his Son cleanseth us from all sin." 1 John i, 7. Does he sigh over his want of conformity to God? He is assured that, beholding as with open face in a glass the glory of the Lord, he shall be changed, (*κατοπτριζόμενοι*, or metamorphosed,) into the same image from glory to glory, even by the Lord the Spirit. (2 Cor. iii, 18.) Does he doubt whether this is *his* great privilege? Again the Spirit speaks in his word, "Faithful is he that calleth you, who also *will do it.*" 1 Thess. v, 24. He is led thus to see that, such is the amplitude of the provision, such the all-cleansing power of the blood of Christ, such the almightiness of the Eternal Spirit, no matter what he may be, the work can be done; and whenever, at any stage of the believer's experience, his faith lays hold of these great promises and provisions, the work will be done. According to his faith it will be done unto him. This work of *entire* sanctification, we see, is the completion of an on-going process of grace in the soul—the entireness of a work which had hitherto been partial, the perfection of a work which up to this point had been imperfect or incomplete. That the work of grace in the soul up to this period may be, and is, *gradual* in most instances cannot be doubted. It is possible for a person subsequently to his conversion to "press forward toward the mark of his high calling in Christ Jesus," "to grow in grace, and in the knowledge of our Lord Jesus Christ," to be maturing and ripening for glory. Probably this is the experience of most of the children of God. Multitudes who are and have been ultimately saved in heaven have never distinctly experienced, or professed to enjoy, entire sanctification. To argue that those only have been saved who have had such definite experience, would exclude the vast majority of all the Church of God. No; the work of sanctification in the human soul may be, and in the majority of instances up to this period in the history of the Church is, *gradual.*

But here I inquire, Can this work of the Comforter be wrought *instantaneously?* May the believer now present his body a living sacrifice, holy and acceptable to God, and be conscious that God now accepts his sacrifice? May he *now* "reckon himself as indeed dead unto sin, and alive unto God through Jesus Christ our Lord?" May the corruptions and impurities of his soul now be all washed away in the blood of the Lamb? May he now, by the aid of the Comforter, measure up to the divine requirement to love the Lord God with all his heart, soul, mind, and strength? To all these inquiries I am constrained, in view of the clear and unequivocal testimony of the word of God, to answer, Yes! O how many dear Christians, not only of the Calvinistic, but also of the Wesleyan belief, halt, hesitate, and stagger just here! How many grieve the blessed Comforter by their doubts, reasonings, philosophizings, and unbeliefs, and enshroud their minds in mist often so dense that all truths are seen in a dim, shadowy, and spectral form by the mind!

The idea that we must wait until death before this work can be done is dishonoring to the blood of Christ and the power of the Holy Ghost. If sin were a material or physical thing, and if its seat were in the body, then death might have something to do in its destruction; but it is in the soul, and death cannot touch it. O it is "the blood of Jesus which cleanseth us from all sin!" It is the Holy Ghost who sanctifies the soul. And if it is the blood of

Jesus which does this work, it can do it *now;* if it is the Holy Ghost who sanctifies, he can do the work now as well as a century hence. But it is so natural for us to ignore the work of the Comforter, and to undertake a legal process, or to look to secondary causes for its accomplishment. We think sometimes a long period of sickness would accomplish it, or some heavy disaster would wean us from the world and make us submit to Christ fully; or, mayhap, if we could be placed in some coveted position in life we might then enjoy and retain this grace. But all this is only "limiting the Holy One of Israel." That the Comforter can, and often does, make use of such means as I have referred to, cannot be doubted. And yet, have we not often wondered at ourselves in coming out of such periods of affliction and trial, or after having been placed in the positions so eagerly desired by us, to find how little spiritual improvement we have realized? But we can no more mortify, or fast, or work ourselves into sanctification than we can into justification. It was not Luther's and Wesley's and Whitefield's fastings and prayers and good works which brought them into a justified state, but it was *faith*, simple faith in Christ, which, by a single act, placed them where months, and even years, of earnest and honest effort had utterly failed to bring them. If we believe, then, distinctively and fully for this great blessing, the Comforter will honor our faith by imparting it to us now.

3. This work of the Comforter in the sanctification of the believer is *distinct* from the work which he wrought in his regeneration. It is not *separated* from it—it was germinally and potentially present then ; but in character and chronologically it is distinct, just as the completion of a work is distinct from its commencement, as death is distinct from dying, as learning to read is distinct from learning the alphabet, or as the bringing on the top-stone is distinct from the foundation of the building. The work of regeneration and initial sanctification is the basal work of the whole Christian character. No one can be sanctified *wholly* who has not been sanctified in part in regeneration, and who is not living, at the time he seeks to have this work wrought in him, in a justified state. To seek sanctification without the enjoyment of justification would be as vain as to attempt to roof a foundationless house. If, therefore,

one would enjoy the *fullness* of God's salvation, he must first have "*tasted* and seen that the Lord is gracious." He cannot be consciously sanctified unless he definitely and distinctly seek for it and definitely and distinctly believe for it. Thus seeking, and thus believing, he will clearly and distinctly receive this grace.

4. The Comforter bears his witness to his operations in the soul at every stage and in every degree. I know there are many who deny the witness of the Spirit to the complete sanctification of the believer on the ground that there is no direct Scripture testimony upon it. It is here distinctly admitted that there is no *direct* revelation upon this point. But the analogical argument, sustained as it is, and has been for a century or more, by the clear experience of many of the most eminent Christians, is both clear and convincing. Now that the Comforter *could* as well bear witness to this work when wrought in the soul as to the fact of our justification will be readily admitted. The only question is, *Will* he do it? Does he ever bear this witness? I have said that the Comforter does witness to his own work, whatever that may be, in the human soul. For

instance, he convinces the world of the ungodly "of sin, righteousness, and judgment"—that is, he so acts upon the soul of the sinner as to produce a sense of sin, "of bondage unto fear." In other words, he bears witness in his soul, not only to his sinful character and condition, but also to the multitude of his sins and the necessary and fearful consequences outflowing from them. When, thus awakened and convinced, the sinner seeks for pardon, he is justified freely and adopted into the family of God, and the "Spirit bears witness with his spirit that he is a child of God." So, as we have seen, the Spirit convinces the believer of the remaining corruptions in his heart, and of his need of purity—of holiness—and inclines him to seek after it. Then, when by faith he grasps the promised blessing, and the work is actually accomplished, the Spirit bears his witness to that work. Hence we see that from the first movements of the Comforter upon the soul, until he finishes his great work of grace, his constant testimony is borne. To the sinner he is "the Spirit of bondage again to fear." To the justified and adopted believer he is "the Spirit of adoption." And to the sanctified believer he is "the Spirit of holiness." To say that the Holy Spirit only witnesses in the soul to our adoption, is contrary to the express teaching of the Word of God. The Saviour distinctly promised, "He shall testify of me," John xv, 26; "He shall glorify me: for he shall receive of mine, and shall show it unto you," John xvi, 14. The Apostle Paul declares that the Holy Ghost gave his attestation to his utterance of burdened desire for the salvation of his "brethren, his kinsmen according to the flesh." "I say the truth in Christ, I lie not, my conscience also bearing me witness in the Holy Ghost." Rom. ix, 1. And the beloved John declares, "Hereby we know that he abideth in us, by the Spirit which he hath given us." 1 John iii, 24. Of course, wherever this witness is, it will be corroborated by the testimony of our own spirit, and by the saintliness of the life of the wholly sanctified one. The two witnesses—that of the Spirit of God and of our own spirit—are always conjoined, and thus the joint testimony is indubitable.

It may be asked here, "If the Comforter has wholly purified and hallowed the soul, is there any further work for him to do?" Most certainly there is. In fact, the soul now, with all its volitions, affections, and intellectual powers, is so completely under his control that he can lead it onward and upward, nearer and still nearer to God in accelerated motion from day to day. Disencumbered of its load of corruption, it rises to loftier altitudes of holiness and love. The believer now "walks with God." His communion with him is sweet and uninterrupted; his peace is calm, deep, settled; it is "*the peace of God*," "perfect peace," and it "*keeps* his heart and mind through Christ Jesus." Love now sits enthroned within his soul, and sways its gentle scepter over all his "passions and his powers." Thus his upward flight is steady, unspasmodic, and rapid.

"Changed from glory into glory,
Till in heaven he takes his place;
Till he casts his crown before Thee,
Lost in wonder, love, and praise."

CHAPTER XV.

THE COMFORTER RESISTED, QUENCHED, GRIEVED.

NO truth is more clearly made known to us in the word of God than that which teaches us that man is the subject of Divine influence. Two things are predicated of this :

First, that this fact is *universal.* "He shall convince *the world* of sin, of righteousness, and of judgment." "That was the true Light which lighteth *every man* that cometh into the world." John i, 9. "The grace [or gift] of God that bringeth salvation hath appeared unto *all men,* teaching us," etc. Titus ii, 11, 12. Even where the light of the Gospel does not shine, and the institutions of the Gospel are not enjoyed, there the Spirit acts directly upon man's heart and conscience, writes the law of God upon his mind, gives him the sense of sin and of the need of forgiveness. Hence, wherever man, redeemed man, is, there the Comforter is at work upon his heart and mind.

Second. This Divine influence is imparted *unconditionally* and *irresistibly*. It is the free, universal gift of God, secured by the atonement of Christ and his mediation before the throne. "The gifts and calling of God are without repentance," (Rom. xi, 29,) or any other condition whatsoever, on the part of man. Just as soon as an immortal being opens his eyes to the light of this world he is encompassed by the gracious provisions of the atonement of Christ. He exists as a redeemed creature, he lives in a redeemed world, in a world where the Holy Spirit is ever employed to bring man back to his God; and, whether he desires it or not, whether he is willing or unwilling, still the Comforter comes to him with his heavenly illumination, his divine influence, convincing him of sin, and of his consequent need of the mercy of God. May I not truly say that man really has no choice in this matter as to whether he will or will not have this divine influence upon his soul? *He is, he must be,* enlightened and convinced "whether he will hear or forbear," whether he will be saved or damned. He cannot prevent the entrance of the Spirit into his heart.

But now, these points being settled, the question arises, "How far will the Holy Spirit exert his sovereign power for the purpose of saving him?" That he is unconditionally and irresistibly *convinced of sin* we have already seen; but will he be unconditionally and irresistibly *saved?* A full answer to this would involve the whole question of the freedom of the human will, which would carry me very far beyond the purpose of this work. There are some points, however, which lie directly in my path, and I proceed to consider them.

1. The precise point where divine agency ends and human agency begins can never be seen by the human eye or expressed in human language. The acutest intellects have expended their utmost strength upon these questions during the by-gone centuries, and the results of their efforts have been unsatisfactory to themselves and to others. There are difficulties involved in all such investigations which can never be fully overcome. While the general statements of the word of God are clear and explicit, yet there are facts in human experience which baffle our chosen theories, and humble our pride into the very dust. It is by

no means infrequent that persons trained under the influence of Arminianism tell us of a period when "they were so wrought upon by the Spirit of God that they could not resist his power," that it was "impossible for them to shake off the influence which had seized hold upon them;" and in the language of the hymn so frequently used,

> "The more I strove against its power
> I felt its weight and guilt the more,"

have expressed their conscious inability to get rid of their burden. Persons in many instances, and in various conditions and circumstances of life, have thus been seized upon, and not only when they have least thought upon the question of their salvation, but also when they have seemed to be the farthest away from God. Their subsequent life of devotion to Christ has given clearest demonstration of the reality of the work wrought in them. On the other hand, the experience of a majority of Christians teaches that, when convinced of sin by the Holy Spirit, they had the consciousness of a power by which they might have resisted this influence, but which they did not will to exercise, but that rather they were inclined to yield to this divine influence and be saved.

Now I ask, *Could* the first class of persons referred to have resisted the Spirit? Could they have *so* resisted him that they would not have been saved? Is their language in the relation of their experience to be taken according to its literal meaning, or as merely expressive of their deep conviction of sin, combined with a willingness on their part to yield to Christ? Who can so answer these questions as to relieve the mind of all doubt concerning them? There is yet another question here, If some men have these deep and overpowering convictions, why do not *all* men have them? That there is a difference of operations we all know, but why is one irresistibly drawn to Christ, and another able to resist so far that he ultimately perishes in his sin and guilt? Volumes have been written in reply to these questions, and the mind is very far from being clear in its conclusions upon them. Where we cannot penetrate it is better for us to bow down and adore.

2. While very many questions which might be asked are thus vailed in obscurity, God's

word clearly and distinctly informs us that multitudes of persons have resisted, quenched, or grieved the Spirit, so that they have ultimately perished ; and thus we learn that the sovereign, eternal, almighty Spirit may be so resisted or quenched or grieved that the design of his operations will be unaccomplished, and man, the subject of these influences, be abandoned by him to endless destruction. Now very early in the history of the world, in fact in its very infancy, God most clearly announced this truth to man : "My Spirit shall not always *strive* with man." Gen. vi, 3. Nevertheless one hundred and twenty years of respite and effort were enjoyed by the antediluvians before the final destruction came. During all that period Noah preached, and the Spirit strove with man ; but never were efforts for the good of the race more persistently or more universally resisted, until finally "the flood came and took them all away." 1 Pet. iii, 18–20. How many of those who struggled and were swallowed up in the seething waters were saved, if any, I have no means of knowing. The Prophet Isaiah declared of the Jewish people, "But they rebelled, and vexed his Holy

Spirit: therefore he was turned to be their enemy, and he fought against them." Isa. lxiii, 10. *Again, Zechariah says of the same people,* "Yea, they made their hearts as an adamant stone, lest they should hear the law, and the words which the Lord of Hosts hath sent in his Spirit." Zech. vii, 12. The martyr Stephen also charges them with the same thing in his address before the Sanhedrim, "Ye stiff-necked and uncircumcised in heart and ears, ye do always resist the Holy Ghost: as your fathers did, so do ye." Acts vii, 51. The same truth is taught in the following exhortations of the apostle: "Grieve not the Holy Spirit of God, whereby ye are sealed to the day of redemption." Eph. iv, 30. "Quench not the Spirit." 1 Thess. v, 19. There can be no doubt that when the Spirit sheds his light upon the mind, and exerts his power upon the soul, it is for the purpose of man's salvation. Without such divine operation he could not be saved, with it he may be saved; but if man resists this influence, and just as long as he does so, he will remain unsaved. If during the whole period of his probation he continues to resist, he will, he *must*, perish; but if he perish at last he will be left without excuse, because all the aid essential for his salvation was imparted to him by the Holy Spirit.

3. There is no portion of the word of God which, if properly understood, teaches that man *will be so irresistibly wrought upon by the Holy Spirit that he will necessarily be saved.* Those portions usually relied upon in proof of such a position really teach no such thing. This language, which, however, is not in the Bible, is often used as a quotation from the word of God to sustain this necessitarian view: "My people shall be *made* willing in the day of my power." This is a misquotation. The language is, "Thy people shall be willing in the day of thy power." Psa. cx, 3. The words implying compulsion are inserted in the passage by the advocates of this view; but suppose they were there, it says nothing about *sinners* being made willing to be saved, but simply, "Thy *people* shall be willing." The Hebrew word employed here, נְדָבוֹת, signifies "free-will offerings," and is the most expressive word in its root and in its various branches of voluntary sacrifice and service in all the language. So it is used in the following passages: Judg. v, 2, 9; Exod. xxv, 2; xxv, 21,

29; Neh. xi, 2; 1 Chron. xxix, 5, 6; Psa. cxix, 108. Again, the language of the Saviour is often quoted for the same purpose: "All that the Father giveth me shall come to me." John vi, 37. There can be no doubt of this. But the question is, Who hath the Father given to the Son? Is it not those whom the Father foreknew as believing on his name? And all who believe on him do and will come to him. Again, Christ says, "No man can come to me, except the Father which hath sent me draw him." John vi, 44. But this does not imply that he will be irresistibly *dragged* unto him. Yet another passage is quoted to sustain the view now opposed: "Work out your own salvation with fear and trembling: for it is God which worketh in you both to will and to do of his good pleasure." Phil. ii, 12, 13. From this it is argued that God so irresistibly works upon man's will that he is necessitated to perform his good pleasure. But certainly the apostle teaches no such thing. He is urging the Philippian Christians to work out their salvation, and for the purpose of encouraging them he assures them that God is working in them "to will and to do of his good pleasure." The natural and legitimate idea is, God gives us the power to will in the direction of our salvation ; but it is for us to exercise that power. He gives us the power to do his good pleasure, but we are to employ that power. Just as he gives us the power to see, to walk, and to hear, while all these faculties are to be exercised by us. We reach, then, the conclusion, that while the Spirit of God strives with every man, yet that there is in man the fearful power of resistance, which he, in very many instances, employs, and that he may so employ it as to render of no salutary effect all the efforts which he makes for his salvation.

CHAPTER XVI.

THE SIN AGAINST THE HOLY GHOST.

WE find in the word of God several important and startling announcements, which, while differing in their forms of expression and in their application to individual character, yet evidently refer to the same sinful acts, their unpardonableness and their irredeemableness. The first is as follows: "Wherefore I say unto you, All manner of sin and blasphemy shall be forgiven unto men: but the blasphemy against the Holy Ghost shall not be forgiven unto men. And whosoever speaketh a word against the Son of man, it shall be forgiven him: but whosoever speaketh against the Holy Ghost, it shall not be forgiven him, neither in this world, neither in the world to come." Matt. xii, 31, 32; (Mark iii, 28, 30; Luke xii, 10.) The passage in St. Mark is similar, but adds to the threatened impossibility of forgiveness, "Is in danger of eternal damnation;" and a sentence of explanation, " Because they said, He hath an unclean spirit." The apostle, writing to the Ephesians, says of some, " Who being past feeling, have given themselves over unto lasciviousness, to work all uncleanness with greediness." Eph. iv, 19. Again, to Timothy he says of certain ones, " Now as Jannes and Jambres withstood Moses, so do these also resist the truth : men of corrupt minds, reprobate concerning the faith." 2 Tim. iii, 8. The same is said of apostates : " For it is impossible for those who were once enlightened, and have tasted of the heavenly gift, and were made partakers of the Holy Ghost, and have tasted the good word of God, and the powers of the world to come, if they shall fall away, to renew them again unto repentance ; seeing they crucify to themselves the Son of God afresh, and put him to an open shame." Heb. vi, 4–6. Again, in the same epistle he says, " For if we sin willfully, after that we have received the knowledge of the truth, there remaineth no more sacrifice for sins, but a certain fearful looking for of judgment and fiery indignation, which shall devour the adversaries." Heb. x, 26, 27.

The Apostle John evidently refers to the

same sin when he says, "If any man see his brother sin a sin which is not unto death, he shall ask, and he shall give him life for them that sin not unto death. There is a sin unto death : I do not say that he shall pray for it. All unrighteousness is sin : and there is a sin not unto death." 1 John v, 16, 17. Jude seems to regard the same character when he writes, "For there are certain men crept in unawares, who were before of old ordained to this condemnation, ungodly men, turning the grace of God into lasciviousness, and denying the only Lord God, and our Lord Jesus Christ. . . . These are spots in your feasts of charity, when they feast with you, feeding themselves without fear : clouds they are without water, carried about of winds ; trees whose fruit withereth, without fruit, twice dead, plucked up by the roots ; raging waves of the sea, foaming out their own shame ; wandering stars, to whom is reserved the blackness of darkness forever." Jude iv, 12, 13.

Some of these passages have, doubtless, a reference to total apostasy from the faith of Christ, and from a state of regeneracy, and others to those who, although unregenerate, yet have rejected the clearest evidences of the truth of Christianity, and by determined and persistent unbelief have placed themselves in a condition beyond the reach of mercy and salvation. It is important that we have, if possible, a correct view of the classes of persons to whom these Scriptures refer. For want of this many have been driven into the deepest wretchedness and gloom, some have been driven into despair and insanity, and some to suicide. Various theories have been entertained of this sin. Irenæus regarded it as the rejection of the Gospel of Christ, and applied it to the Gnostics; Athanasius believed that it consisted in a denial of the divinity of Christ; Origen thought that it was any mortal sin committed after baptism; Augustine applied it to every one who died impenitently.

The most commonly received opinion of modern times is, that this sin consists in attributing the miracles wrought by Christ to Satanic agency, when, according to their own belief, the casting out of devils could only be accomplished by the Spirit of God. This opinion seems to have some foundation in the following language. Our Saviour on the occasion now referred to had just cast out a devil, blind and dumb. At this marvelous manifestation of power the *people* were amazed, and inquired, "Is not this the son of David?" "But when the Pharisees heard it, they said, This fellow doth not cast out devils, but by Beelzebub the prince of the devils." In replying to this our Saviour said: "If I by Beelzebub cast out devils, by whom do your children cast them out? therefore they shall be your judges. But if I cast out devils by the Spirit of God, then the kingdom of God is come unto you." Matt. xii, 24, 27, 28. Now it is evident from this language that the Saviour did primarily declare that the Pharisees on this occasion had committed this sin.

1. Before this time they—the Pharisees—had taken some interest to inquire as to his character and his mission. At a very early stage of his ministry they were anxious to learn who and what he was. But their carnal expectations of a Messiah were not met in him. In their pride they had looked for one who should come in power and great glory, in all "the pomp and circumstance" of an earthly conqueror, and that the outcome of his appearing would be

their disinthrallment from the bondage of Rome, and their establishment as the rulers of the world. This idea had been ingrained in the very heart of the Jewish nation. Even the disciples of our Lord clung to it until after his resurrection from the dead, and it was only burned out of them by the pentecostal fires. Thus, while the Pharisees might have been willing to receive him as a great teacher, or even as a great prophet, they would not receive him as the divine Messiah. Had his great power been exerted in behalf of their temporal aggrandizement they might, and probably would, have hailed him as their king. But he made it plain to them that he would not do this—that this was not his purpose—and, consequently, they rejected him. Now, having as a body resolved upon rejecting him, their course, or line of conduct, was marked out ; they would by some means, sooner or later, compass his death.

2. Their first efforts were to be directed against the influence of his miraculous works. It is a remarkable fact that the first attack of the enemies of Christ in all the ages has been against those miracles which furnish a demonstration of his divinity. That he did wonderful

works, all acknowledged. The people saw these works, and believed that they were wrought by the power of God. The Pharisees reasoned, therefore, that the people must be induced to take a different view of them or they would never be able to succeed in their sanguinary purpose. The occasion for making a demonstration in this direction soon occurred. A man was brought to Jesus who was blind and dumb, and he healed him. The people at once were impressed that Christ was indeed "the Son of David." The Pharisees, as we have seen, heard this inquiry. Now was their time. They therefore said to the people aside, "He casteth out devils by Beelzebub, (or Beelzebul,) the prince of the devils." In other words, He is in league with Satan to deceive the people.

But the omniscient Jesus, although they had said this aside when they thought that he did not hear them or know what was in their thoughts, proceeded to answer their vain, unfounded, and wicked assumptions. Now it was in view of this state of things that Jesus said to them, "Wherefore"—in answer to what you have said, and as a result of your saying—"I say unto you," etc.

3. It is evident that this was no sudden ebullition of feeling on the part of the Pharisees. It was not uttered in a moment of excitement, but it was a premeditated thing, and undertaken with the design of undermining the authority of Christ among the people. They had made up their minds deliberately to reject him—to put him to death. But they wanted the people with them. From the very first the masses had heard him gladly. They had followed him in vast throngs to the mountain, the sea-shore, and the desert ; they had hung upon his lips as he uttered his loving words, and had stood in wonderment and awe in the presence of his stupendous miracles. It would seem, therefore, that the Pharisees had resolved on one of those three expedients, or upon all of them : Either they must turn the people against him, or they must put him to death privately, or they must so involve him with the Roman government as to insure his death as a traitor to that government. They were now trying the first of these expedients, and hence they came out thus boldly and blasphemously.

4. I do not think that they committed the unpardonable sin by merely saying what they

said. But the utterance of their lips was only the outward evidence of the state of their hearts. It was in their hearts before it passed their lips. They had determined upon saying this as soon as the occasion should arise; and just as soon as that occasion arrived they said it coolly and deliberately, and, I may add, maliciously. It was not, then, the isolated utterance which brought upon them this terrible announcement; it was not this alone which sealed their doom: it was their willful and determined rejection of Christ, which, ere their lips had uttered these blasphemous words, had cut them off from all hope of salvation. The utterance was only the outcropping of their unbelief and wickedness—only the legitimate fruitage of their corrupt hearts. It was the outward demonstration of their deep and damning depravity. Hence Christ immediately adds: "Either make the tree good, and his fruit good; or else make the tree corrupt, and his fruit corrupt: for the tree is known by his fruit." And again: "O generation of vipers, how can ye, being evil, speak good things? for out of the abundance of the heart the mouth speaketh." Matt. xii, 33, 34. It is a very slight and shallow view of this question which many take, that the unpardonable sin consisted in the outward act alone. No, their unpardonableness and consequent future damnation were the result of their rejection of the Son of God.

5. Now, then, as the immediate result of their change of attitude toward Christ, his course was changed toward them. He soon speaks to them in parables, which they, in their blindness, would not, and could not, understand; which he knew they would not understand, and, may I not add, *which he designed they should not understand.* How terrible is the significance of the language of Christ against them in private to his disciples when explaining to them his parables! "Therefore speak I to them in parables: because they seeing see not; and hearing they hear not, neither do they understand. And in them is fulfilled the prophecy of Esaias, which saith, By hearing ye shall hear, and shall not understand; and seeing ye shall see, and shall not perceive: For this people's heart is waxed gross, and their ears are dull of hearing, and their eyes they have closed; lest at any time they should see with their eyes, and hear with their ears, and should understand

with their heart, and should be converted, and I should heal them." Matt. xiii, 13–15.

All his subsequent utterances to the Pharisees were in threatenings, denunciations, and woes, while they in their willful and confirmed unbelief were hurrying on to meet their final and irrevocable doom. They had taken their position. *Christ must die.* And failing to get the people with them, and fearing to put him to death themselves, they involved him by forsworn witnesses with the Roman authority, and by wild and persistent clamors they induced a weak and wicked Roman Governor to deliver him to be crucified. A few short years only passed away, and the wrath came upon them to the uttermost. Their city was taken, their temple destroyed, and the blood of the murdered Christ, which in their fearful imprecations they had invoked upon themselves and upon their children, was visited on them until more than a million of the Jewish people perished, and the historian tells us that more were condemned to be crucified than they could obtain crosses to place them on. As they had willfully rejected Christ there was no further sacrifice for their sin, and only a "fearful looking for of judgment and fiery indignation." Heb. x, 27.

But the question arises here, *Is it possible for any one now to commit a sin that is unpardonable, and that will place him beyond the reach of hope and mercy?* I answer, Undoubtedly it is. But let it be remembered that this is not a sin which stands out isolated and independent of all other actions, but which is rooted deep in pre-existing depravity, unbelief, and sin. It is, indeed, the culminating act of a series of transgressions rashly persisted in for a longer or shorter period. It is a final act, which links itself to a long chain, and completes the work by which the soul binds itself to an endless perdition and irredeemable woe. "The principal misunderstanding of this passage has arisen from the prejudice which possesses men's minds owing to the use of the words, 'The *sin* against the Holy Ghost.' It is not one particular act of sin which is here condemned, but a *state* of sin, and that state a willful and determined opposition to the present power of the Holy Spirit." *

Before proceeding further it is well now to

* Alford *in loco.*

determine the meaning and force of the word "blasphemy" in the passage under consideration. "When the word," says Mr. Webster, "is used in reference to men it signifies injurious and calumnious speaking, reproachful speeches made against them. When it is applied to God it signifies not only reproaches uttered against him, but also a denial of the attributes and excellences he possesses, and includes always the idea of willful and rebellious enmity." Lange, in his exhaustive commentary, says, "It is open and full opposition to conversion, and hence to forgiveness. The Holy Spirit, who is here spoken of in distinct terms, is the last and highest manifestation of the Spirit of God, who completes and perfects the revelation of God, and in that capacity manifests himself in the human consciousness. Blasphemously to rebel in opposition to one's better knowledge *and conscience against this* manifestation and influence of the Holy Spirit is to commit moral suicide, and to destroy one's religious *and moral susceptibility*." *

In view of these definitions and explanations I am now prepared to say,

* **Lange** ***in loco.***

such is not the case. The very facts that they are still anxious about their souls, that they tremble under the apprehensions of approaching judgment, that they would fain come to Christ and enjoy the favor of God, that they regard his forgiveness and his favor as the most desirable things in the universe—all give evidence that *they may be forgiven.* True, their sins may be great ; they may have often resisted the Spirit ; their transgressions may be multiplied and aggravated ; but if they *desire* forgiveness, that evinces that the Spirit of God is still influencing their hearts and inclining them toward Christ. And just as long as the Holy Spirit remains with the sinner he may be saved. Those who have committed this sin have no more feeling or concern about their souls. They are "past feeling." The darkness has become so dense that the light of the Spirit fails to penetrate it. Conscience has become so seared that it is unreached by the agencies of redemption, and its voice no longer thunders down through the avenues of the soul in tones of warning and alarm, and the heart is so incrusted in ungodliness and unbelief that nothing affects or moves it. Let me say, then, dear reader, if still you weep, and feel, and pray, whatever other sins you may be guilty of, they are not unpardonable. *There is forgiveness for you.* It is wonderful that God *can* forgive such a sinner; but he *can* and he *will* forgive you if you will now heartily accept of Christ.

4. While the tokens of perdition may be apparent in some persons, yet it would be difficult, and, indeed, impossible, for us to say of any one that he is guilty of the unpardonable sin. There may be in our minds an awful fear that such sin has been committed by some person or persons whom we may know; our vitals sometimes almost freeze with horror as we think of such a possibility in their case; but we cannot say with certainty that such *is* the case. God does not place the flaming seal of his condemnation upon the brow of the doomed man so visibly in this world that mortal eyes can clearly discern it. We may have thought that we could almost trace the fiery characters written there, and yet some of whom we have thus thought have subsequently had the name of the Lord written there. And there may be others, for whom we are fondly cherishing hope, who are going about with their doom written upon their souls. One

thing is clearly evident, namely, that every time the Spirit is quenched or grieved, man takes another step toward this fearful state. Every time, in fact, that he resists the gracious influences which are brought to bear upon him for his salvation he is hastening the fatal catastrophe. He may, by timely repentance, avoid the fatal crisis ; he may reach it ere he is aware. Every unconverted man should tremble and stand in awe in view of the fearful peril of his position. He stands in jeopardy every hour, not only of death, but of what is worse than a thousand deaths—*abandonment of God.*

It is impossible for any finite being to know precisely how or when this crisis may be reached, or to see definitely where lies the boundary line between mercy available for pardon and salvation and the wrath of God, from which there is no escape. There can be no doubt, however, that God does all he can do, consistently with his character and man's moral agency, for the salvation of each individual soul, and that no one goes down to the abodes of sorrow and despair until Infinite Wisdom clearly foresees that any further effort for his salvation would be utterly unavailing. It is then that the ever-deepening darkness of an endless night—starless, rayless, hopeless—settles down upon the deathless soul, now forever abandoned of God. No words can express this more fully than the following lines, written by Dr. Alexander:

"There is a *time*, we know not when,
  A *point*, we know not where,
That marks the destiny of man
  To glory or despair.

"There is a *line*, by us unseen,
  Which crosses every path;
The hidden boundary between
  God's *patience* and his *wrath*.

"To pass that limit is *to die;*
  To die as if by stealth;
It does not quench the beaming eye,
  Or pale the glow of health.

"The *conscience* may be still at ease,
  The spirits light and gay;
That which is pleasing still may please,
  And care be thrown away;

"But on that forehead God has set
  Indelibly a mark,
Unseen by man, for man as yet
  Is blind and in the dark.

"And yet the doomed man's path below
  Like Eden may have bloomed;
He *did not*, *does not*, *will not*, *know*
  Or *feel* that he is doomed.

"He knows, he feels, that all is well,
  And every fear is calmed;
He lives, he dies, he sinks to hell,
  Not only *doomed*, but *damned*.

"O where is this mysterious bourne
  By which our path is crossed—
Beyond which God himself hath sworn
  That he who goes is lost?

"How far may we go on in sin?
  How long will God forbear?
Where does hope end? and where begin
  The confines of despair?

"An answer from the skies is sent,
  'Ye that from God depart,
While it is called to-day repent,
  And harden not your heart!'"

"AWAKE, thou Spirit, who of old
Didst fire the watchmen of the Church's youth,
Who faced the foe, unshrinking, bold,
Who witnessed day and night the eternal truth;
Whose voices through the world are ringing still,
And bringing hosts to know and do thy will!

"Oh that thy fire were kindled soon,
That swift from land to land its flame might leap!
Lord, give us but this priceless boon
Of faithful servants, fit for thee to reap
The harvest of the soul: look down and view
How great the harvest, yet the laborers few.

"Oh haste to help ere we are lost!
Send forth evangelists, in spirit strong,
Armed with Thy Word—a dauntless host,
Bold to attack the rule of ancient wrong;
And let them all the earth for Thee reclaim,
To be Thy kingdom, and to know Thy name."

BOGATZKY, 1690.

CHAPTER XVII.

THE COMFORTER AND THE MINISTRY.

IT is said that the Prussian embassador at the Court of St. James, during the reign of Frederick the Great, wrote to his royal master complaining that, while other ministers rode to court in their carriages, and with liveried servants, he was obliged, in view of the smallness of his salary, to ride in a hackney-coach. To this the king, who was parsimonious in every thing else except his army, replied, "Never mind; when Cousin James sees you coming, he always thinks he sees me just behind you with a hundred thousand of my Prussians."

The idea present to the mind of the king was, that however poor, and even shabby, the external circumstances of his embassador might be, he was backed up by a power which no earthly government would care to provoke. Without such a power vain were splendid coaches, liveried servants, and all the insignia of embassadorial rank. With such a power all these things sank into comparative insignificance.

This suggests to us the true point of view from which we are to regard the Christian ministry. Without the presence and power of the Almighty Comforter, vain are all merely external aids and appliances. With this power, they may not only bid defiance to earth and hell, but may succeed grandly in their great work. While the feet of the Lord Jesus were still pressing the brow of Olivet, ere he had begun his "great ascent," he said to his wondering disciples, "*All power* is given unto me in heaven and in earth. *Go ye therefore*, and teach all nations." Matt. xxviii, 18, 19. It was in view of this that he declared unto them, "Ye shall be baptized with the Holy Ghost not many days hence." And again, "Ye shall receive power, after that the Holy Ghost has come upon you." Acts i, 5, 8. It was in view of this, also, that they were commanded to tarry in the city of Jerusalem until they were "endued with power from on high." Luke xxiv, 49. Without this power he knew that they were nothing, and that they could do nothing; with it they were to shake the world, and "turn it upside down." This power was not natural to them, nor inherent in them ; it was supernatural, superhuman, superangelic ; it was *divine*. It is evident, therefore, that the ministry of the Church are utterly powerless in the accomplishment of their great work unless called to, and qualified for, and mightily aided in it by the presence and power of the Holy Ghost.

1. The *call of the Comforter is essential to warrant any person to undertake this work.* No man has the right to take upon himself this office and work unless he be thus called by the Holy Ghost. No one can make choice of the ministry as he would of a trade, or of the profession of medicine, of law, of science, or of arms. The ministry is not really a *profession;* it is a *calling*. Many, doubtless, regard it and enter upon it as a profession ; but this is a perversion of the design of the great Head of the Church. Men who thus enter the ministry will never do much in the accomplishment of its great work. They may go through its round of duties perfunctorily, but they will never really build up the Church, or bring souls to Christ. God has never delegated the work of choosing his min-

isters to any man or any company or class of men in the world. He calls his own ministers, he appoints his own embassadors; and these are, very frequently, the persons whom the wise and prudent of this world would pass by. It was not the rulers in Israel—the rich, the wise, the mighty—that the Son of God called to be his apostles, but the humble fishermen of Galilee. And the greatest reformers, the brightest luminaries of the Church, have had a humble origin: Luther, the son of a forgeman; Melanchthon, coming forth from an armorer's shop; Calvin, not the son of wealthy, although of respectable, parents; Whitefield, the son of a poor innkeeper; and the Wesleys, the sons of a poor minister of the Church of England. Thus it has always been; so it is now. But the humbleness of their origin, the unpropitiousness of their circumstances, the deficiencies, in some instances, of mental culture, and the rudeness of the speech of some, have been more than compensated for by this mighty endowment. Splendid natural gifts, superior elocutionary powers, the silver tongue of eloquence, the graces of oratory, the vast and varied stores of learning, are all well; they are all to be desired, under certain conditions. But neither of them, nor all of them combined, will go to make up a minister *of* Christ, nor *for* Christ. "Not many wise men after the flesh, not many mighty, not many noble, are called: [" call you."—*McKnight*:] but God hath chosen the foolish things of the world to confound the wise; and God hath chosen the weak things of the world to confound the things which are mighty; and base things of the world, and things which are despised, hath God chosen, yea, and things which are not, to bring to naught things that are." And why is all this? "That no flesh should glory in his presence." 1 Cor. i, 26–29. Nor is it sufficient, even, that a man is a Christian, and in the enjoyment of the grace of God in his soul, although this is indispensable for the one who is called into this work. But it is not every Christian whom God calls to the higher ministries of his Church. Every Christian, it is true, is called upon to testify for Christ, to bear witness in honor of his name; and, in the New Testament sense, every Christian is a prophet or a preacher; but all are not called to devote themselves exclusively to this work.

This is a point which cannot be too carefully guarded at this time. Now when the laity of the Church are awakening to a sense of their duties and responsibilities; when the obligations to speak for Christ seem to weigh heavily upon many hearts; when the spirit of testimony is given to multitudes of the servants and handmaids of the Lord, care should be taken lest they should, in the heat of their zeal, attempt to obliterate the distinctive call of the Comforter to the office and work of the ministry—lest they should say, with Korah, Dathan, and Abiram, "Ye take too much upon you, seeing *all* the congregation are holy, every one of them, and the Lord is among them." Num. xvi, 3. Although all the people of the Lord in a sense are holy, yet all are not called to this responsible work. The Church may appoint its officers, its Sunday-school teachers, and other helpers; but she has no right to set apart any man to the work of the ministry, unless he is especially moved by the Holy Ghost. It may be said that, doubtless, many persons are mistaken in their convictions about a call to the ministry. This may be so, but they need not be mistaken. The inward call to this work stands not alone;

it is always confirmed by corroborative testimony which need leave no room for doubt. If there *is* room for reasonable doubt on this matter, a man should hesitate long before he takes upon himself this office, if, indeed, he is warranted at all to take it upon him. But where there are good natural gifts, where there is undoubted piety, where the Holy Spirit puts his seal upon the incipient efforts of the one who feels that he is called to this work, where the eye of the Church recognizes these things, and her voice calls him to devote himself to preaching the Gospel—he who thus enters upon this life-work may be well assured that he has not run before he was sent. If all these things combine to call him to this work, then "woe is unto him if he preach not the Gospel." If, however, he lacks the inward call, and the outward corroborative testimony, let him abide in his calling, whatever it may be, and there work and speak and live for Christ.

2. But when a man is thus called by the Comforter to engage in this work he will realize that his continued presence and power are essential, not only to give him a *fitness* for it, but also *success* in it. It has been well said by

Mr. Arthur, "If the preaching of the Gospel is to exercise a great power over mankind, it must be either by enlisting extraordinary men, or by the endowing of ordinary men with extraordinary power.* It is ever to be borne in mind that the great design of the Christian ministry is twofold: first, to bring lost men, perishing and dying men, to Christ; and, secondly, when they have come to Christ and have been saved by his grace, to build them up in holiness, and love, and faith. Now unless these designs are realized by the professed minister of Christ, and in so far as they fail of being realized, just so far forth is his ministry a failure; a failure, mayhap, not for want of sincerity, not for want of culture, not for want of labor, and not even for want of both mental and physical energy; but a failure for the want of power, of spiritual, divine power. The "midnight oil" may be expended in the elaboration of his sermons; all the stores of knowledge within his reach may be ransacked to enrich and adorn his productions; he may be earnest in his delivery, cogent in his reasonings, and splendid in his imaginings; and yet his sermons, although "faultily

* Tongue of Fire, p. 97.

faultless" and "icily regular," may, in their moral effects, be "splendidly null." "We may stand and gaze," says an eminent writer, "upon the Aurora Borealis, as it spreads over the heavens pure as the blushes upon an angel's face, and yet we grow cold as we gaze."* So many a heart grows cold toward God and Christ, as the flashes of intellect or genius dazzle the imagination or please the fancy.

And, right here, I would ask in all honesty and sincerity, Are not many of our Churches at the present day making a great mistake in their hot haste after men of genius, star-gazers, flashing meteors, who shall, by their oratorical powers, their oddities and eccentricities, or mental aberrations, attract a gaping crowd, fill empty pews, and stuff empty contribution boxes? "Verily" such Churches "have their reward." Is it not true that any Church, under ordinary circumstances, may be crowded, and any ministry made successful, if that ministry is baptized with the Holy Ghost, and that Church is in earnest in its great work? Is it not to be feared that such ministers as I have referred to are sought for the purpose of *supplementing* the

* Dr. Todd.

declining liberality and the withheld labor of a cold and frozen Church ? And is it not true that, under the given conditions, all the seeming growth and prosperity of such Churches is only *seeming*, without any real foundation, and utterly at the mercy of certain adventitious circumstances ?

But on the other hand, where the ministry are anointed with the Holy Ghost, and the Churches are earnestly co-operating with them, there will be real prosperity, substantial growth. There the people will say, "God is with you of a truth." This anointing, or endowment, or baptism, of the Comforter will not make men great in the ordinary and accepted sense ; but it will make them good, it will make them men of power, of usefulness, and of great efficiency in the kingdom of God. O it is one thing to preach the Gospel without the Holy Ghost, and another thing to preach it "with the Holy Ghost sent down from heaven !" Look at the great difference in the disciples of our Lord after they had received this baptism. While the Master was with them, there was not any thing very remarkable which they either said or did. When he was arrested, they all forsook him and fled. Peter was cowed before a servant-maid, and his countenance was blanched with fear as he muttered oaths and curses in his denial of Him whom he had promised only a few hours before to follow even to prison and to death. But only fifty days have passed, and behold the change! Right in the midst of the city of Jerusalem, right in the face of the Jewish Sanhedrim, right in the face too of imprisonment and death, they boldly preach "Jesus and the resurrection." And Peter, who had been the cowardliest of them all, charges the Jews with the murder of the Son of God, while he offers them life and salvation through his blood. And see, while he speaks, while he quotes one Scripture after another, every eye is fixed, every tongue, for the while, is silent! Then a tremor of horror runs through their veins as the conviction that they have crucified the Son of God flashes upon their minds. Then their bosoms begin to swell and heave with sorrow as the heavens grow black with wrath over their guilty heads, and the terribleness of their sin is revealed to them. At length they can restrain their pent-up feelings no more, and a wild, piercing cry, a wail bursts forth simultaneously from thousands of immortal beings, "Men and brethren, what must we do?"

Now I would not say that results of equal magnitude will always accompany the gifts of the Comforter. The Church, strictly speaking, has never had but one Pentecost. The same conditions do not always exist, and, indeed, these conditions under which the Gospel is preached are always varying; but I do say that similar results in their character will, *must*, follow such a divine baptism. No instance of failure is on record. The number of the saved may be greater or less, but some will be saved. How some ministers can go on from year to year in a dull routine of duty, and yet see no results of their labors, is a marvel to heaven and a triumph for hell. How they can be satisfied, how they can rest by day or by night, how they can *live*, is more than we can comprehend. Then, again, there are some ministers who are keenly alive to their duties and responsibilities. They have entered the work of the ministry from the purest of motives, and under a deep, all-absorbing consciousness of a divine call. They are earnest men; they preach with their might; they study long and hard;

they are diligent in their pastoral work, and of course they have measurable success ; but they are conscious of a great lack somewhere in their ministry. They are not the men of power that they want to be. Their usefulness is very far below what they feel it ought to be. They often ask themselves, "Why is it so? I study, I labor, preach, visit, pray, and the Lord of the vineyard knoweth that I am sincere, that I want to glorify him only ;" but they ask, with many groans and tears, "Why am I not more useful? Why do I not bring more souls to Christ?" Their closets are vocal with their sighs and groans, and bedewed with their tears. What shall they do? They can study with no more earnestness than they have, they can employ no more physical energy than they have done, for perhaps even now they are worn and wasted by their exhausting efforts. In their agony, at times, they would that the Master would release them from their work either by calling them home, or by allowing them to engage in some secular employ.

To such a one I would say, "My distressed brother, your condition calls forth my most hearty sympathies ; but allow me kindly to call your attention to the very thing which you lack, giving you credit, as I most certainly do, for all honesty and sincerity of purpose, and fidelity in labor; yet one thing thou lackest." Do you ask me, "What is that?" I answer, "The *full baptism of the Holy Comforter.*" I do not mean to say that you have not the Comforter. You have him with you. He bears witness with your spirit that you are a child of God, and his comfort, peace, and joy are yours. Nor can I doubt that you have been called by him to this work; but, mayhap, for the want of a clear appreciation of your privilege, for the want of an appropriating faith—or, to come still closer home, from an unwillingness to pay the price and to accept the responsibilities connected with this gift—you are not in the enjoyment of such an endowment of power as it is your privilege to possess. This is what you want, and this is *all you want.* And this you may have to-day, *now.* Even now the Divine Comforter is hovering over you; even now the divine baptism is ready to descend. Are you ready to comply with the conditions? to put yourself in an attitude to receive it? Do you ask, "What must I do?" I answer, "Make a complete surrender of yourself, your will, your reputation, your ambition, your all to Christ. Consecrate all to him forever, and then believe that your heaven-ascended, glorified Christ *will* bestow upon you this gift; that it is his good pleasure to do it, and that he will do it now." "And will he do it? Yes, blessed be his name! he will."

But it must be remembered that this gift will not be bestowed upon any one for his personal gratification, or to satisfy his ambition, or to make it appear that he is something great. If it is bestowed it is to make us personally holy—to make us useful to others; while all shall see that it is not a power, or a strength of our own by which the results following are realized, but that "the excellency of the power is of God." O if we would only put ourselves into connection with this power, how mightily God would work in us and by us! And if all the ministers of the Lord Jesus were thus anointed they would shake all the continents and islands of this globe! A moral resurrection would stir and startle this whole valley of death, and an exceeding great army would be raised up for the service of the Lord our God. And is it not the will of God that *all* his ministers should be thus endowed? Is there any thing lacking in the provision for this gift? Is there any limitation in the promise? Is there any thing in either the provision or the promise that would hinder any of us from receiving the gift now? If not, the hinderances, the barriers, must be all in us. But we may remove them all by the aid of divine grace. Let them, then, be removed, and the living fire will descend, the pent-up waters will flow freely.

In the possession of this power what wonderful results have already been realized in the history of this world! The day of Pentecost and the city of Jerusalem were not the only time and place when and where these great results have been witnessed. In Rome and Corinth, in Philippi and Thessalonica, in Ephesus and Galatia, similar effects were produced, until the triumphs had become so general, so uniform, and so widespread, that the apostles joined in one grand pæan: "Now thanks be unto God, which always causeth us to triumph in Christ, and maketh manifest the savor (odor) of his knowledge by us in every place." 2 Cor. ii, 14. The whole Roman empire felt the impulse of this moral movement; the idolatries of Egypt, Greece, and Rome were swept away before its onward progress. Mooned Ashtaroth was vailed, and Osiris was heard no more in Memphian groves.

> "Peor and Baalim
> Forsook their altars dim;"

The mount of gods was shaken as by an earthquake; the thunder fell from the powerless hands of Jupiter; the helmet fell from the brow of Mars; the trident dropped from the dripping hand of Neptune, and the charms of Venus faded away forever. Even the oracles of Delphi and Dodona were struck dumb. It was in view of this that Milton sang:

> "The oracles are dumb;
> No voice or hideous hum
> Runs through the archèd roof in words deceiving;
> Apollo from his shrine
> Can now no more divine,
> With hollow shriek the steep, of Delphos cleaving.
> No nightly trance or breathèd spell
> Inspires the pale-eyed priest in his prophetic cell."

But these were only external manifestations of this divine power which was moving upon the hearts of millions. The apostles of our Lord were not personally and directly iconoclasts. They did not go with ax and sledge-hammer to the temples of idols, and hew or break them down from their thrones or their pedestals; but, aided and empowered by the Comforter, they did go directly to human hearts and consciences; and when idolaters were converted and saved they first deserted, and afterward destroyed, the idols which they had formerly worshiped. And where are now the thirty thousand divinities of Egypt, Greece, and Rome? Where, indeed, have they been for the last fifteen centuries? They have literally "perished from off the face of the earth." And they have so perished that they could never be restored, nor their worship and service revived. All the power of Julian the Apostate was not sufficient to restore the speech of the oracle at Delphi, or to uprear the fallen systems of idolatry which the "preaching of the Gospel, with the Holy Ghost sent down from heaven," had destroyed.

The reformers in the sixteenth century were endowed in like manner, and, consequently, their triumphs were great. It was not in their own strength that Huss and Jerome were enabled to "witness a good confession," and that the last-named went to the stake singing, "*Salve feste dies!*"—"Hail, festal day!" It was not by his own might that Luther stood like a

"Tower impregnable to earth and hell."

It was the power of the blessed Comforter which nerved the sweet, gentle Melanchthon to stand up amid the fiery storm of persecution, scattering the rays of heavenly truth around him while he lived, and in his dying moments to reply, when asked if he wanted any thing more, "*Nihil, nisi cœlum*"—"Nothing, unless it be heaven." This upheld Calvin in the midst of his persecutions, and of all the herculean labors which he performed for Christ's cause. This made John Knox more terrible to Queen Mary than an army with banners. And was it not this which winged the fiery logic of John Wesley with irresistible power, and inspired the sweet poetic strains of his brother Charles? And was it not this which melted the heart of Whitefield with sorrow and love, and enabled him to bring thousands down into the dust at the feet of Jesus? The co-laborers of these saintly men, and multitudes of their successors, have been animated, inspired, and empowered by the same Almighty Agency.

All the men of superior wisdom and might

under the Old Testament dispensation, who did great things for God and his cause, were said to be animated and inspired with the Holy Spirit. It was he who dwelt in Joseph, giving him illumination and understanding; that upheld and directed Moses in the difficult and ofttimes embarrassing positions which he occupied, and who rested upon the seventy elders, so that they also prophesied. He inspired Bezaleel to construct the tabernacle, and Solomon to build the temple. Joshua was "full of the spirit of wisdom;" Othniel and Gideon, Amasai and Zechariah were "clothed with the spirit;" David, Elijah and Elisha, Jahazael and Jehoiada, Isaiah and Jeremiah, Ezekiel and Daniel, and all the prophets, were inspired by his divine influence. "So that we have," says a recent writer, "more than *eighty* distinct notices of the presence and power of the One Eternal Spirit before the evangelical effusion of the Holy Ghost." *

Now the word of God warrants us to believe that the Comforter is even now ready to produce equal, and even grander, results than have ever yet been accomplished, if we will only use

* Spirit of Life, p. 23.

the ordained means to secure his sovereign agency. There is, there can be, no lack of power in the Comforter. Nor is there any lack of *willingness* on his part to reproduce these triumphs upon an enlarged scale, and with mightier demonstrations. This is, emphatically, his dispensation, and we are living at what would seem to be the culminating period of this dispensation. And can we suppose that there is to be any lack of energy or of efficiency in his operations? On the other hand, are we not warranted to believe that there will be more wonderful forth-puttings of his power? Is not the page of revelation luminous with the glowing prophecies and promises of the glory of these latter days? Is not the Comforter ready to come down upon his ministers and his Church in richer, fuller, deeper baptisms than have ever yet been received? O then we are not straitened in him, but we are straitened in ourselves! Our views are narrow, puerile, and unworthy. We act from motives unworthy of our high vocation. We too often seek to *please* men, when we should be in an agony to *save* them. We "court a smile, or woo a grin, when we should save a soul." We do not pray for great things;

we do not believe for great things, or expect great things. And "according to our faith, so it is unto us." Many are pigmies when they might be giants. We are weak as other men, when we ought to be shaking down, bending, and breaking the very pillars of Satan's kingdom. O that all the Christian ministers of America, and of the world, were clothed with the same spirit that the old prophets were clothed with, that the apostles were clothed with, and that our fathers possessed! If, then, ye ministers of the Lord Jesus, it is your *privilege* to have this Spirit, and to strive with the hosts of hell "according to his power who worketh mightily" in the believer, is it not your duty to enjoy this gift, this divine endowment? If you are remiss when you know what is your privilege and your duty, will you not be accountable for your remissness? The question comes home now to the heart of every minister, "Are you willing to pay the cost of such a baptism? Are you willing to accept the responsibility of receiving such a baptism? There is not, I believe, a minister in the land but who would be willing *to have* this power; yea, farther, who is not desirous to have it. But are you willing, ye consecrated sons of Levi, to have this gift in God's appointed way? True, our heavenly Father gives the Holy Spirit to them that ask; but how are we to *ask?* In faith, certainly. But we know well that the exercise of faith is conditioned upon the pre-existing state of the mind and heart. For instance, Jesus said, "How can ye believe that receive honor one from another, and not the honor which cometh from God only?" How, indeed, can we believe if we cherish any darling idol which we refuse to surrender; whether it be self, pride, reputation, ease, honors, family, position, or whatever it may be? There must be a complete surrender of our all, an entire submission to God, and a willingness to be any thing that he would have us be. I would not say that we are to be willing *to be nothing*. Alas! too many are willing, in a sense, to be nothing—nothing, that is, either great or good in the kingdom of God. We would be great in the estimation of our fellow-men. We want to occupy great positions. We want to preach great sermons. And there are some, it may be, who would willingly have this power if it would advance their interests in these directions. But all this must be given up, and the soul must come down into the dust of the deepest self-abasement, and the lowest humiliation before God, if we would have this baptism of power. Yes, we must "ask in faith, nothing doubting." That faith must recognize our deep, pressing need of this baptism ; a need so seen, so *felt*, that we shall cry mightily unto God for it, and never rest until the gift is ours. This faith must also recognize that it is the will of the Father, and of the Son, that we should have the gift, and have it *now*. We know that the Father is ready, that the Son is ready, that the Spirit is ready, and that the promise is ready. My brethren in the ministry, *are we ready?* Suppose that the rushing fires of another Pentecost should now come upon us, are we prepared to accept the responsibility which that Pentecost baptism would bring with it? God does not squander his gifts. Now, this baptism of the Spirit enables a man *to be* what otherwise he could not be, *to do* what he could not do without it, and to think and speak as nothing else could enable him to do. There comes, then, with this supernatural endowment a vastly increased responsibility to think and speak and do as God would have us. There is, indeed, a consciousness within the soul of this power, and along with that comes the divine requirement to act up to the full measure of our acquired ability.

It was so with Isaiah when the living flame brought by the seraphim had "touched his lips, and taken away his iniquity, and purged his sin." Instantly he hears the voice of the Lord saying, "Whom shall I send? and who will go for us?" And immediately he replied, "*Here am I; send me.*" And never was there prophet or minister sent upon a more fearful mission. "And he said, Go, and tell this people, Hear ye indeed, but understand not; and see ye indeed, but perceive not. Make the heart of this people fat, and make their ears heavy, and shut their eyes; lest they see with their eyes, and hear with their ears, and understand with their heart, and convert, and be healed." Isa. vi, 9, 10. Without a moment's hesitation he went, and the recorded result of his mission made by himself is, "All day long have I stretched out my hands unto a disobedient and gainsaying people." And then, after having completed his mission, after having uttered God's message in sweetest and sublimest words, he was sawn asunder, and his seraphic spirit winged its flight to the realms of endless day. He did not begin to comprehend, when the vision of the glory of the Lord burst upon him in the temple, what was the design of God with reference to him, what he was to do, and what he was to suffer; but he readily accepted the divine commission with all its fearful responsibilities. We might be willing to accept this endowment of the Comforter if we knew that it would lead us to a career of great prosperity and usefulness, and thus increase both our efficiency and our prominence; but to go forth and labor without great, visible, tangible results, to be persecuted and despised, to be little and unknown, to suffer, mayhap *to die*, for the Lord Jesus—it is from such results that we shrink. Perhaps even now, coming, as some one may, to the very threshold of this baptism, he is ready to shrink. His mind is suggesting innumerable difficulties, and Satan is near to magnify those difficulties to the uttermost. He is standing, halting, trembling, doubting, fearing. But I would say to that one, Let the question now be settled. It has been *the* question of your religious, your ministerial, life.

Now then say, "At whatever cost of sacrifice and suffering, whatever responsibility this baptism may bring with it, I will, *I must have it.*" There is only step more. Believe, and the promised gift is yours, the power is yours; the Comforter comes, and not only is every avenue of the soul made luminous with his glory, but its every power is girded with his strength. Do you ask, "What am I to do with this gift?" I answer, "Use it, use it freely, use it constantly." The source whence it comes will never fail you, for it is infinite, it is inexhaustible. It has been well said that "The natural effect of such a blessing would be moral strength, certainty, courage." It makes the "righteous man as bold as a lion." It "sets his face like a flint." And if this power is in the soul it will be seen and felt in its wonderful effects. Not only will its possessor be conscious of its presence, but those to whom he ministers will see and feel that "God is with him of a truth." And here, dear ministers of the Lord Jesus, is what the Church wants, and what the perishing world around us imperatively demands.

There is no doubt of the general correctness of the old adage that "Truth is mighty and will prevail." But God has promised and pledged a power to accompany the truth, to give it demonstration and efficiency in the accomplishment of his great designs. This gives to the truth its effect upon human souls in convincing, regenerating, and sanctifying them. This, this is absolutely necessary for this work, and this we may have in all its richness and fullness even to-day. Shall we have it?

CHAPTER XVIII.

THE COMFORTER AND THE CHURCH.

OF the one hundred and twenty who received the pentecostal baptism only twelve, including Matthias, were apostles; the rest were brethren and sisters; but the "cloven tongues sat upon *each* of them," and "they were *all* filled with the Holy Ghost." So with those assembled at the house of Cornelius, when they believed the word which was spoken by Peter: "The Holy Ghost fell on all them which heard the word." Acts x, 44. And in the narration of this event which the apostle made in the Council at Jerusalem he says, "The Holy Ghost fell on them as on us at the beginning." Acts xi, 15. Thus it was every-where. Believers of every condition in life, and of every grade of intelligence, received the wonderful gift. The promise of the Comforter is unlimited to any age, or country, or clime, or condition in life. It is to "even as many as the Lord our God shall call." Acts ii, 39. It is to us and our children as much as to those who were present in the upper room, or who were present in Jerusalem at Pentecost. If, therefore, any one is destitute of this gift it is either because of the want of a clear appreciation of his privilege, or of an earnest, believing effort to enjoy it. No language could possibly be clearer or more explicit than that in which this promise comes to us, and we are living at a period of the world's history when the Church may confidently expect more abundant outpourings of the Spirit than at any former period of its history. It is in these last days that the Spirit is to be poured out upon all flesh; that our sons and daughters are to prophesy, our young men to see visions, and our old men to dream dreams; that the Spirit is to be poured out upon the servants and handmaids of the Church, that they may prophesy. (Acts ii, 17, 18.)

In the early Church all possessed this gift to a greater or less degree; but the gifts of the Spirit—his extraordinary gifts—were not alike in all. "There are diversities of gifts, but the same Spirit." I. Cor. xii, 4, 11. All even then did not have "the gift of healing," all did not "speak with tongues," all did not "work miracles," all did not "interpret;" but all were "filled with the Holy Ghost." It was this which constituted them living members of the body of Christ, living branches of the living vine; it was this which made them laborers together with God, and which gave their labors such wonderful success; it was this which enabled the Church to shake the world, and "turn it upside down." But when error blinded its sight, and a mass of forms and ceremonies stifled its breath, and a rush of worldliness paralyzed its energies, then it was bereft of its supernatural strength, and, like the shorn Samson, both feeble and blind, it became the sport and the prey of its enemies. Like a wire disconnected from the battery, or the wheel, with the stream turned away, or shut off, from its buckets, or the train loosed from the engine, or the body separated from the soul, so the Church, separated from the Source of its power, became not only inadapted to its work, but, also, incapacitated for its performance. Here and there individual souls maintained the connection, and experienced and manifested the power derived therefrom; but the body at length became a putrefying mass, a rotten carcass, over which the eagles of destruction swooped, and deep into which they plunged their curved beaks.

The Reformation era witnessed the re-awakening of men's minds to the great, although long unknown, truths of God's word. Then there was a trumpet-blast which rang out clear and strong among the Alps, the Pyrenees, and the Appenines, and reverberated from the chalky cliffs of Britain's isle, calling upon the nations to arise and shake off the blinding dust of the ages from their brows, and to snap the fetters which had so long bound them in civil and ecclesiastical bondage. The nations, responsive to the call, "leaped to loose their chains." The light of the truth, which had been concealed by the thick, massy clouds of superstition, ignorance, and error, again burst forth, and the nations exultingly shouted as they beheld its radiance. Just as the inhabitants of hyperborean regions, when a night of many months is about to pass away, assemble upon some mountain-summit, ready to hail with joy the first appearance of the sun's disk emerging from the wintry night above the horizon, as the first faint rays betokening his approach are seen, send up a loud shout which is caught up over all the realms where darkness had so long held unbroken sway; so the nations, when they saw the first rays of eternal truth, hailed them with rapturous joy as the harbingers of an approaching day of brightness and glory. But great and glorious as was the work accomplished by Luther and his co-laborers, it was not, after all, a revival of pure, spiritual religion. It brought out clearly some of the great truths of God's word, and especially that of justification by faith. It furnished the great basal truths to the masses which were afterward to be employed in the revival of a pure, spiritual Christianity; but it was hindered by fearful conflicts with the civil powers, by wranglings about mere words, and forms, and ceremonies, by an alliance with the State, and by retaining many things which still had "the smell of Rome upon them." It was not until after a two-century baptism of fire, and blood, and death, that some of the ministry and laity of the Church began to see clearly the need of a revival of spiritual religion. The "Holy Club" at Oxford, while prayerfully studying that Bible which was henceforth to be their "one book," saw their privilege in Christ Jesus, saw the promises at first dimly; but after fasting and praying and struggling for weary days and months, the clear light shone upon their souls, and another Pentecost came upon Europe and America. The people were now taught, as they had not been since the apostolic days, *that every one who believed* should receive the gift of the Holy Ghost, regenerating their souls, bearing witness to their sonship and heirship, sanctifying them wholly, and transforming them after the image of the heavenly and the divine. Soon the pulsations of a new life began to beat and throb among the masses, and a revival of spiritual religion was begun, which is still going on, and which will continue until millennial glory bursts upon the world.

And yet, after all, while the results of that revival have been of the most glorious character, the Church, as a body, does not understand, or measure up to its privilege. What now I would say to every Christian is, "You may receive the gift of the Holy Ghost, and enjoy his agency in the complete salvation of your soul, and in a full "preparation for every good work" This is your blood-bought privilege, your heavenly birthright, the ascension gift of your Lord." More willing—how *much more* an archangel could not tell—than evil, earthly parents are to give good gifts unto their children, is he to give this blessed Comforter to you, and to give him to you now. Are you ready now to open your hearts and receive the heavenly Messenger? He will only come to dwell in your hearts when you feel the need of him, and earnestly ask him to come. He will only *abide* with you if you will not quench his light, or grieve him, so as to cause him to take his departure.

1. It is clearly evident now *that the condition of the whole Church imperatively calls for this gift of the Comforter.* While great things have been accomplished during the past century under the new Pentecost which came upon the Church at its dawn, all earnest Christians are deeply impressed with the need that its members have of aiming at a higher position, and occupying a higher platform of spiritual experience and of spiritual power. This is the greatest present need of the Church. This can in no sense and to no extent be supplemented by the multiplication of material agencies ; nor can

they substitute this gift. A large increase of wealth, of numbers, of church edifices, of institutions of learning, is a great cause of rejoicing, if it is looked to only as a *means* and not as an *end.* But if we look upon these things with a self-satisfied complacency, and look no farther and no higher, then decline, decay, and death will fasten upon the very vitals of the Church. A mighty politico-ecclesiastical institution, like the Roman Catholic Church, may be consolidated and perpetuated by superstition, by appeals to the prejudices and passions of men, and by keeping their minds in bondage. But the destruction of such an institution is only a question of time. It is only "the word of the Lord which endureth forever." "And this is the word which by the Gospel is preached unto the people." A long career of prosperity in the Protestant Churches of Christendom has given to them wealth, numbers, social position, civil power, and world-wide respectability. And in many instances these things have acted fearfully against them. Wealth has given rise to pride, luxury, fashion, worldly-mindedness, covetousness, love of forms and ceremonies; and these have, in some instances, smothered, and in others eaten out, the very life of the Church. Many so-called Christian Churches are the very centers of fashion ; in fact, they take delight in being known as "fashionable Churches." The assemblies which gather in them on the Sabbath present rather the appearance of a "dress parade" than of companies of Christian worshipers. Mammon, fashion, lust, are worshiped by the thoughtless, giddy, flirting throng. The idea of a spiritual religion is scouted by the pulpit and the pew as the very essence of fanaticism and folly. There is only now and then a minister so far gone toward rationalism or Rome as to denounce "Protestantism as a failure," but instances of this kind have not been wanting. I admit that the cases referred to above are exceptional, but that they exist none can doubt ; and they are fearful, wicked caricatures of the religion of the Lord Jesus. But, I ask, is it not true that in very many of our Churches these worldly influences are exerting their power ? Has not this mania for dress, and fashion, and show, seized upon many of the people professing godliness ? Are not vast sums, incalculable in their amount, annually expended for the gratification of this passion ? Are not the mouths of many ministers closed upon this subject for fear of giving offense to their rich and fashionable members? Now what is to check, ay, and roll back, this in-rushing tide of worldliness? This enemy to spiritual religion is "coming in like a flood." What, or who, but "the Spirit of the Lord can lift up a standard against him?" But not only so. While the very life of many of our Churches is being assailed in this way, Romanism on the one hand, and infidelity in its thousand forms on the other, stand ready to assault, and hope to carry our works, and to sweep the Church of Christ from the earth. Yea, more. While we are dallying with our Delilahs, and parleying traitorously with our enemies, immortal souls, treading with rapid and fearful strides the broad and beaten highway to hell, are leaping from its fearful precipices into the rayless darkness of an eternal night. Surely, then, we cannot doubt the necessity of a marked and wonderful outpouring of the Holy Spirit.

2. This is also needed, not only that we may maintain our present status of benevolent and evangelistic efforts, and our contributions toward the various enterprises of the Church, but,

also, that we may go forward to meet the demands which are so urgently pressing upon us. Under the revival influences of the last century the liberality of the Church has increased more than a thousandfold. In fact, during the last half century most of the benevolent enterprises of the Church have been born and carried forward to their present gigantic proportions ; but the providence of God is opening up new fields of enlarged dimensions, and is calling upon the Church to lift up its eyes and see them white already to the harvest, and waving to the sickle of the reaper. Now a religion which utterly ignores all creature merit, no matter of what sort it may be, can never call forth for any length of time large benefactions, unless it is actuated by the spirit of Christ and inspired by his bright and lustrous example. If man can be made to think that his contributions and his works will entitle him to eternal life, and will give him indulgence to live as he lists in the present life, then he will give his money without stint or measure. This is the grand lever by which the Romish Church lifts such vast sums of money for the purpose of carrying on her operations. This has given her the control at various periods of the moneys and estates of nations and of kingdoms. But Protestantism presents no such plea; it desires to present no such plea. Its claims are based upon Christ's commands, his promises, and his example, and it regards and teaches that the love of Christ is the strongest motive and most controlling principle which can call forth the liberality and the labors of his people.

But if this love decline, if the throne where Christ should reign unrivaled is usurped by the world, then the heart will shrivel under the new reign, its warmth will be chilled and congealed, its views will become warped and narrowed, and the cause of Christ will be permitted to languish and decline. Thus we see that the presence and power of the Comforter are not only needed for our spiritual life, peace, and joy, that we may be enabled to live a holy life, that we may instrumentally bring souls to Christ; but, also, that the spirit of liberality may be maintained and greatly enlarged, until every human habitation has been visited with the light of the Gospel, and every human heart has tasted and tested its power.

3. The promised presence of the Comforter

is needed in our Churches, that their members may be able to furnish a *living exemplification of the religion of Christ.* The Church is "the light of the world," "a city set upon a hill," to be seen by, and to give light to, all that are around. It exists for the illumination and salvation of the world. The preaching of the Gospel, the circulation of the Scriptures, the instruction of the people in religion both publicly and privately, are valuable and ordained means for the upbuilding of the kingdom of Christ; but nothing can compare in its efficiency to the practical, living demonstration of a holy life to convince the gainsayer, and to show to the world that there is a divine reality in the religion of Christ. The world does not go to the Bible, or to institutes of theology, or to any of the mighty tomes which have been written in defense of Christianity, to learn what religion is; but it expects that every one who professes to be a Christian shall furnish a specimen of what it is, and of what it can do for an immortal being; and it has a right to expect this. The great Teacher himself has said, "By their fruits ye shall know them." "Men do not gather grapes of thorns, nor figs of thistles." So the great apostle to the Gentiles acknowledges the fact and the value of such evidence when he says, "Do we begin again to commend ourselves? or need we, as some others, epistles of commendation to you, or letters of commendation from you? Ye are our epistle written in our hearts, known and read of all men: forasmuch as ye are manifestly declared to be the epistle of Christ ministered by us, written not with ink, but with the Spirit of the living God; not in tables of stone, but in fleshy tables of the heart." 2 Cor. iii, 1–3. Every Christian then should be an epistle of Christ, known and read by men, and declaring to all what the religion of Jesus can do for a poor, fallen, ruined, and guilty sinner. The great purpose of constituting the Church of Christ in the world is that its "light may *so* shine before men that they may *see* its good works, and thus be led to glorify our Father who is in heaven." If men profess to be Christians, and live like other men—are as vain, proud, ambitious, covetous, over-reaching in business, or dishonest in their dealings—then the natural, the legitimate, result will be that the world will not only disbelieve in religion, but will come ultimately to despise its very name. Of all the arguments which infidelity has adduced in its conflicts against the truth of God, none have been so difficult to deal with, and none have been plied with a greater efficiency and a more alarming success, than the one arising from the inconsistent, irregular, and often hypocritical conduct of many of its professors.

Nothing has so much power to shut the brawling mouth of infidelity as the consistent, devoted life of the follower of Christ. *A holy life is an irresistible and unanswerable argument for the truth and reality of the religion of Christ.* Such a life cannot be manifested unless it be as a result of the mighty transforming and sanctifying grace of the Comforter ; but if it were generally exhibited to the eye of the world it would effectually stay the floods of Rationalism, Pantheism, Socialism, and the thousand kindred antagonisms of our holy Christianity. With this power the Church could resist them all, as the rocky cliff resists the rushing, roaring waves of the sea, and breaks them into foam at its feet. This is a living, visible testimony, which all the negations of skepticism and its bitter hatred of truth are incapable of resisting. There are some men who will scoff and sneer at Churches, and creeds, and Christians in general, but the mere mention of a father's prayers, and of a mother's counsels, tears, and devoted piety, will hush their clamors, and bring burdened tears to their eyes. But without the indwelling Comforter men cannot live this life of devotion to Christ, and exemplify the principles and the power of his holy religion. They may endeavor to imitate it, they may strive to galvanize their dead souls into something resembling this divine life, but all their efforts will prove abortive, and result only in their confusion and disgrace. And while this cannot be successfully imitated, neither can it be compensated. Christ's kingdom is not of this world. It is a divine, a spiritual kingdom; it is "righteousness, and peace, and joy in the Holy Ghost." Such a kingdom can only be maintained and extended by spiritual agencies. Physical agencies, "bodily exercise," gorgeous rituals and ceremonials, may help to maintain a sensuous religion; but only the Holy Ghost can make living Christians, and through them bring this redeemed world to Christ.

4. *This is all which the Church now needs to*

complete its grand mission in the world. I have said that this baptism of the Comforter is all that the Church needs; I now say that it has this in a measure. What is wanted is the fullness of this grace and power. The machinery of the Church, all its means and appliances, is well-nigh perfect. The strategic points which have been seized upon in the great battle-ground of the world are all that could be desired. There is wealth enough and there are numbers enough to speedily conquer this world for Christ; and, added to all this, are the grand preparations which Providence has been making during the roll of the centuries in leveling the mountains, exalting the valleys, smoothing the rough places, and straightening its crooked ways, so that now the whole world is open to the Gospel. Even Rome, the Eternal City, so long barred against the entrance of the truth, has now been opened in God's providence; the scepter of temporal sovereignty has fallen from the feeble hands of the aged Pontiff, and the complete destruction of the system of which he is the head is not far distant. Now, also, the Bible, that wonderful two-edged sword which proceedeth out of the mouth of the Son of God, is translated into more than two hundred of the languages and dialects of the world, and is ready to exert its power upon a thousand millions of its population. Besides this, the "ends of the world" have evidently come upon us. In this period, the lines of prophecy seem to be converging, and the blush of the dawn of the millennial morning is already upon the face of the sky. What is wanted, then, for the grand consummation of our work in the world? Nothing, I say nothing, but this mighty baptism of the Comforter. "O Christians, is there such a doctrine in our creed as the doctrine of divine influence? Is there such an agent in the Church as the Almighty Spirit of God? Is he among us expressly to testify of Christ? to be the great animating Spirit of his missionary witness—the Church? and is it true that his unlimited aid can be obtained by prayer; that we can be baptized with the Holy Ghost, and with fire? O ye that preach, believe the promise of the Spirit, and be saved! Ye that love the Lord, keep not silence, send up a loud, long, united, and unsparing entreaty for his promised aid! This, this is what we want, and this is all we want. Till this be obtained all the angelic agency of heaven will avail us nothing, and when it is obtained all that agency will be unequal to the celebration of our triumph." *

And this divine, almighty agency which we need, is at our doors, is even now hovering over us. He is waiting, willing, ready now to give to his people such an endowment of power as will completely equip them for this last struggle and prepare them for a final and glorious victory. There is no lack, then, in our machinery, nor is there any want of power in the Comforter. What is needed is that his almighty power should be connected with this machinery. It is not enough that the engine be perfect in its construction, that the steel-plates and brass mountings be well polished, that the furnace be well filled with fuel and the boiler with water. All these conditions might exist forever, and not a motion of the machinery be made. There is another condition yet necessary—absolutely essential, and that, is fire. When that is present all the other conditions begin to be employed. Steam is rapidly generated, and the whole attached train is drawn to its destination, even over the breadth of a

* "Church in Earnest," by J. A. James, p. 267.

whole continent. So the poles for the telegraphic wires may be properly set, and the wires be stretched over mountain and valley, hill and plain, or the cable be laid down in the ocean's depths, and yet no message be borne over them forever ; but now let the battery be attached, let the electric current be brought to bear upon these wires, and messages will be flashed with lightning speed over all the land, down through the coral coffins of the sea, among the sporting monsters of the deep, and over buried argosies, until the whole world is brought into almost instantaneous communication. So now let the connection be formed between the Eternal Spirit and the machinery of the Church, and the whole will be set in motion, and messages of mercy and of salvation will be borne over all lands and over all seas. Still further let me illustrate this in the terse language of an earnest living preacher : "Go into a room where there is a galvanic battery. You see it with its cups and plates and coils and wires apparently perfect. You propose to try its power upon your own person, and so you lay hold of those two shining balls, one with either hand, and wait for the shock ; but you do not feel it.

Then for a moment you imagine you feel its current thrilling your frame, but sober reason says it is not so. You press the balls the harder, as though the vigor of your grasp might give them power, but no answering thrill comes, and you throw them down and seek for the cause of the failure ; when right there in the heart of the machine, where the power should be concentrated, there is no coil, hence no power." * But now let the essential coil be put in its place, let the current be applied, and then take hold of the balls, and every nerve and muscle and fiber of your being will quiver under the power of the battery ; so when these currents of divine influence are brought to bear upon dead souls, ay, when they shall be brought to bear fully upon the whole valley of death, there will be a stir, a noise, a coming together of bone to bone, and a great moral resurrection will be the result. Take one more illustration from the author of the Tongue of Fire : "Suppose we saw an army sitting down before a granite fort, and they told us that they intended to batter it down, we might ask them,

* Rev. W. H. Boole before the New York State Methodist Convention.

'How?' They point to a cannon-ball. Well, but there is no power in that; it is heavy, but not more than half a hundred, or perhaps a hundred weight. If all the men in the army hurled it against the fort they would make no impression. They say, 'No, but look at the cannon.' Well, there is no power in that. A child may ride upon it, a bird may perch in its mouth: it is a machine, and nothing more. 'But look at the powder.' Well, there is no power in that; a child may spill it, a sparrow may peck it, yet this powerless powder and powerless ball are put into the powerless cannon; one spark of fire enters it, and then in the twinkling of an eye that powder is a flash of lightning, and that ball a thunderbolt which smites as if it had been sent from heaven. So is it with our Church machinery at this day. We have all the instruments necessary for pulling down strongholds, and O for the baptism of fire!"—P. 301.

And why should not this baptism of fire now fall upon the Church? Why should all these agencies and means and appliances stand comparatively powerless? Why should not this dead world even now be quivering and shaking with the throes of a new birth, and, bursting its sepulchral womb, come forth into the life, the brightness and glory of the long-promised millennium? It is for the Church to answer why; and although the answer would, doubtless, reveal its sin and shame, it had better be made speedily. Yes, we will answer now: "We have failed to understand our privilege and our duty, or, when we have known our duty, we have either criminally neglected to obtain this gift of power, or, by erecting barriers in the way, we have hindered the application of the power of the Holy Ghost."

5. *Without this baptism of the Comforter the Church will prove itself to be a failure in the sight of angels, devils, and men.* Let me ask, Why was the Church instituted? For what purpose does it exist in the world? What is its mission? Is it not *to evangelize and save the world?* The last command of Christ, ere "the chariots of God" bore him upward to his everlasting throne was, "Go ye into all the world, and preach the Gospel to every creature;" to "teach all nations," or, literally, to make disciples of all nations. And this is not merely or solely the duty of the ministry, but

also, of the whole membership of the Church. Every added member, whether old or middle-aged or young, rich or poor, bond or free, is to be a "*light-bringer* and *a light-bearer*," a preacher of the Gospel, a messenger of mercy to this world. There is, there can be, no exception to this rule. In some way, in some sphere, every one is commanded to labor during the brief day of life's probation in the Lord's vineyard. The Church, then, is designed to be a soul-saving institution, and every Christian is to be a soul-saver; not, of course, efficiently, but instrumentally. The order of the great Head of the Church is universal, exceptionless, differing in its application as widely as are the diversities of character, position, and relation in life, and yet all are to work on in harmony toward the same grand result. Just as in a large cotton factory, there are wheels of almost every size and in almost every position, some nearer to the source of power and some more remote, some more and some less prominent, some visible to the eye of the visitor and others invisible; but amid all the whirl, the confusion, and the noise, there is not one wheel, or spindle, or hand, but which lends to the production of the designed fabric. So, in the Church, diversities of gifts and operations there are, but it is the same Spirit working in all and through all for the accomplishment of his glorious purposes. Who can doubt this? And yet, if it is true, how very far have its members come from answering this design? The activities of the Church in almost every place are confined to the few; the mass of its members are idlers. "The harvest truly is plenteous, but the *laborers* are few." When we ought to be shaking the world, or turning it upside down, we are, too many of us, settled down into idleness and indifference. We are mere pigmies when we ought to be giants; we are dwarfed, stunted, powerless, when we ought to be "mighty through God for the pulling down of the strongholds of sin and Satan." O how long shall this state of things be continued! What can, what will, wake us up from our slumberings and engage us earnestly in the work to which we are called! Will God permit an outburst of persecution to arouse the Church, or will there come down upon its whole length and breadth a mighty effusion of the Comforter? Something must be done, and that right early.

And if the Church fails to answer the design of its existence it becomes only a weak, shriveled, powerless thing. When the living flames expire from its altars, then there will be substituted in their place, for a season, a merely sensuous religion, a merely formal and outward show, and sooner or later will come on a sad degeneracy into error, superstition, strife, divisions, decay, and death. "Christianity, then, would sacrifice its divinity if it abandoned its missionary character and became a mere educational institution. Surely this article of conversion is the true *articulus stantis aut cadentis ecclesiæ*. When the power of reclaiming the lost dies out of the Church it ceases to be the Church. It may remain a useful institution, though it is most likely to become an immoral and mischievous one. Where the power remains, there, whatever is wanting, it may still be said that 'the tabernacle of God is with men.'" *

* Ecce Homo, p. 278.

CHAPTER XIX.

THE DISPENSATION OF THE COMFORTER THE MOST GLORIOUS AND THE LAST.

DURING the four thousand years preceding the Christian era, two dispensations flourished, decayed, and vanished away. Each was preparatory to, and explanatory of, the other. The first was the patriarchal, all dim and shadowy, but adapted to the infancy of the human race. While it lasted, "God revealed himself at sundry times and in divers ways." In two marked instances he revealed his "wrath against the ungodliness and unrighteousness of men." In the one he destroyed the race by a flood; in the other he swept the cities of the plain with a storm of fire. There was also revealed to men the existence of another higher and purer state of existence. Men heard the rustle of angels' wings, saw their bright forms, not only in vision, but actually descending from the heavens, and then returning thither again; but they learned even more of the existence of that higher state of being than this. They probably saw the deathless patriarch go up to the heavens in a chariot of fire, and they knew then that the world whence the angels had come was not only for them, but for men; for the good, the pure, the holy, such as they knew Enoch had been. But above all this, they knew that, although the race was fallen, wicked, and exposed to God's wrath, there was a Redeemer, a Saviour provided, through whom "all the families of the earth should be blessed." The most explicit promises of Him were given to Adam, and repeated to Abraham, Isaac, and Jacob. The coming of "Shiloh," to whom "the gathering of the people should be," was regarded as a certainty, and looked forward to with delight and rejoicing. Thus in the gray dawn of the world's history, the light of God shone upon the pathway of man, revealing himself, his relation to his creatures as their Almighty Sovereign, rewarding the righteous and punishing the wicked, and opening up before his wondering eyes another and a future world.

The prophetical, or Mosaic, dispensation was formally inaugurated upon Mount Sinai in the giving of the law, amid the most terrible and sublime accompaniments. The tabernacle and its worship were formally instituted, and sacrifices, rites, and ceremonies were ordained by the direct command of God. A new and a brighter era had now dawned upon the world. There was now furnished to man not merely a traditional revelation of God, but what was far better for his understanding and use, a *written one*, with all the great truths which he had taught man along the line of the past centuries formally gathered up and recorded in "the book of the law." During the fifteen centuries which followed, a succession of prophets not only foretold the advent of the Messiah, but also the establishment, extension, and glory of his kingdom. And yet, glorious as was this dispensation in all of its external forms, many intimations were given that it was only temporary, that another and a more glorious one was to dawn, erelong, upon the world, and that amid its brightening glories the mists and the shadows were all to pass away. The prophets referred to that on-coming period as "that day," "the last days," "the day of the Lord." At length the tones of the prophetic harp were hushed, and a night of centuries came down upon the Jewish Church, in which no voice of God was heard, and no angelic messengers were seen by man. At the dawn of the morning which followed, and which was ultimately to culminate in the glories of the millennium day, "a voice was heard in the wilderness" uttering the heraldic cry, "Prepare ye the way of the Lord." "Repent, for the kingdom of heaven is at hand." "He is coming whose shoe-latchets I am not worthy to unloose." "He shall baptize you with the Holy Ghost and with fire." He came. His advent was attended by the most remarkable demonstrations on the part of the heavenly hosts, who had in countless numbers sung over Bethlehem's plains, "Glory to God in the highest!" until the very air trembled with the burden of their song, and heaven's high courts were resonant with their exultant shouts. Then, after a few brief notices of him, he is seen no more until he is "thirty years old." At that time we behold him standing upon the banks of the Jordan, ready to be initiated into the office of a priest by one regularly descended from the tribe of Levi, in order "to fulfill all righteousness." The work is done, by what precise form we know not, and then "the heavens are opened, and the Spirit of God, dove-like, descends upon him, while a voice from the opened heavens says, "This is my beloved Son, in whom I am well pleased." Here, then, we behold the whole Trinity—the Son, in human flesh, the Spirit like a dove hovering over him, and the Father speaking from the heavens, bearing his testimony to his incarnate Son. Wonderful scene! Grand inauguration of the Son of God into his priestly and prophetical offices!

His great life-work is now fairly begun, and after forty days of fasting in the wilderness he is brought into immediate conflict with the prince of darkness. Thrice assaulted by him, he is in each assault the victor; the thunder-scarred head of the arch-fiend is bruised by his conqueror, and he receives the premonitions of his final and complete subjugation. Three years of unceasing teaching and miracle-working follow. At length his departure from earth is at hand. Intimations of this fill the hearts of his disciples with sorrow and grief; but he assures them of the coming of "another Comforter, who shall abide with them forever." Then he is taken by his enemies, and "by wicked hands is crucified and slain." But he rises again, and for forty days he appears at intervals to give assurance of his resurrection to his disciples. Then he ascends to his Father and our Father, to his God and our God. He sits down upon his regal and mediatorial throne, the joy of all heaven, the center of its bliss. But he does not forget his disciples who are waiting and longing for the fulfillment of his promise. And when the day of Pentecost has fully come, he sends down the Comforter with all his gifts, his grace, and power.

The new, the Christian dispensation, is now inaugurated. The ceremonial law has evanished, and the moral law exists no more as the ground of man's acceptance with God. The "*do* this and *live*" economy has passed away, and the "*believe* and be *saved*" dispensation is now in force. Panoplied with the might and power of the Divine Comforter, the infant Church sprang at once into the very midst of the arena of conflict with the philosophies, the mythologies, the idolatries, the superstitions, and the wrongs of the world, and with its mighty spiritual weapons began to pull down the strongholds of the kingdom of darkness. Persecuted, hated, imprisoned, butchered, as were its members, yet their numbers increased, and "the word of God mightily grew and prevailed." "But if the ministration of death, written and engraven in stones, was glorious, so that the children of Israel could not steadfastly behold the face of Moses for the glory of his countenance; which glory was to be done away; how shall not the ministration of the spirit be rather glorious?" 2 Cor. iii, 7, 8. But great and glorious as were the triumphs of the early Church, the present day is witnessing scenes which are only equaled, but scarcely surpassed, by them. The dawn of the nineteenth century witnessed the most enlarged preparations for the speedy conversion of the world to Christ. Organizations began to be multiplied for the concentration of the piety, the beneficence, and the labors of the Church. And as its operations were enlarged, and its convictions of duty were intensified, Divine Providence was opening one door after another before its wondering eyes, until now the whole world is open to the messengers of the Gospel. These organizations, as we have seen, were born in the midst of the revival which began in the eighteenth century, and were baptized with the same Spirit who inspired the triumphs of the apostolic age. And under these mighty agencies which have been called into requisition, whole districts of the earth have been evangelized and Christianized. The inhabitants of the Sandwich Islands have been reclaimed from superstition and barbarism, and the last relics of their former idols and idolatrous practices have almost totally disappeared. Their large and flourishing Churches have not only become independent and self-supporting, but, in turn, are sending out missionaries for the conversion of the islands of the sea to Christ. The Fiji Islanders, from idolatry, brutality, and cannibalism, have been brought under the influence of the Gospel, and have sat down at the feet of Jesus, "clothed, and in their right mind." More recently still, the island of Madagascar, where hundreds of the followers of Jesus formerly sealed their testimony with their blood, and had furnished a martyrology which, in many instances, was equal to that of the early years of the Church, has been brought under the power of the Gospel. Its idols have been publicly burned, its bloody altars have been overthrown, its temples have either been deserted and destroyed, or else converted into houses for Christian worship, and its queen has become, in a sense at least, a nursing mother to the Church. In hyperborean regions, as well as on the banks of the Ganges and the Irrawaddy; in Africa and in China, in Turkey and in Hindostan, and, indeed, in most of the languages and dialects of the world, there are tongues which speak the Saviour's praise. But not only so; while this mighty baptism has been upon the Church, and its forward movements have been crowned with such signal success, directly or indirectly traceable to the same influence is the great work which has been wrought in the cause of human liberty. England has emancipated the millions of her slaves; Russia has lifted up thirty millions of serfs from their degraded and enslaved condition; and America, in the midst of a baptism of blood and tears, struck the manacles from the limbs of four millions of slaves, and has since asserted their manhood, and granted to them the elective franchise.

> "The light! the light! it breaks;
> Light on the chain of the slave,
> The light of God on the laborer's home,
> Light on the martyr's grave!"

If this is the last and most glorious dispensation, certainly we are beginning to see the culmination of its glories. Much as has been said of the activities and energies of this age, "the half has never yet been told." There is no man living who is fully capable of grasping in his mind, no matter how enlarged its powers may be, the mighty influences which are at work, and the mighty changes which are, even now, going on in human society. The rapid disappearance of great wrongs which had for ages rooted themselves in the constitutions and governments of the world ; the fading away of idolatrous systems ; the recent overthrow of the temporal power of the Beast, which will be followed ere long by the destruction of the power of the False Prophet ; the multiplication of facilities for the evangelization of the world ; the rapid increase of agencies for this work ; the binding of continents together by rails of iron and steel ; the union of oceans by canals, and the girdling of the earth with telegraphic wires, are all events which in their magnitude and significance are above the comprehension of mere finite intelligences. And yet, grand and glorious as these events are, they do not begin to answer the prophetical descriptions of the full glory of this dispensation of the Comforter.

What we now see is only the dawn of the morning; what the prophets saw in vision was the full glory of the meridian of a day which will fill all earth and heaven with hosannas and halleluias.

This is God's last dispensation of mercy toward our world, and this is rapidly drawing toward its close. The Father has worked, and the Son has worked, and now, for ages, the Holy Ghost has been working. We have not discerned his agency or felt his power as we might have done. But his work, in connection with the redemption of our world, is now being better understood, more fully appreciated, and more heartily trusted in, than at any former period. It only wants that the Church, the whole Church, should cry more mightily to God for the fuller manifestation of the Comforter, and it will be realized in a manner hitherto unknown. "Whatever increase Christ's kingdom has received from the beginning down to these times, it has received through the power of the Comforter; and if it is receiving any at this day, if we find reason to bless God for the manner in which the heathen in any part of the earth are now coming into his kingdom, our especial thanksgiving and praise are due to the Comforter, who is still working his threefold conviction, and casting down the abominations of idolatry thereby." *

And are we not warranted to expect results upon a grander scale than any that have yet been realized? Is it not apparent, from what he has already wrought, that the Comforter "is able to do exceeding abundantly above all that we ask or think, according to the power that worketh in us?" Eph. iii, 20. As yet we have only seen and known a part of his ways; but the fullness, the thunder of his power, who can understand? He has but in a partial manner, and in a few places, displayed his power, and we have lifted up our hands in astonishment and exclaimed, "Wonderful! Wonderful!" But if our faith properly appreciated the work of the Comforter we should not only expect to see these, but also far greater things. O, the time hastens when he will lift the vail from the long blinded mind of the Jewish people, and they shall look upon him whom they have pierced and mourn, "as one mourneth for an only son!" The Beast and the False Prophet

* The Mission of the Comforter. Hare, p. 181.

shall be overthrown and cast into the lake of fire. Idolatry, which, in one form or another, has cursed and crushed millions of the world's population for thousands of years, shall be destroyed, with all its fearful train of superstitions and abominations, its lusts, and its crimes. Intemperance, the vile monster, which has by its arts degraded and ruined millions during the past centuries, shall come to an end, and its power shall be completely destroyed. All forms of vice and iniquity shall be banished from the world, and "righteousness and joy and peace" shall reign for ever and ever. Then "the earth shall be full of the knowledge of the glory of the Lord as the waters cover the sea." No one shall have to say to his neighbor, "Know the Lord: for all shall know him from the least even unto the greatest." Then the luminous and sublime predictions of David, Isaiah, Jeremiah, and Daniel will be fully realized, and the glowing utterances of the Apocalypse will have their glorious completion.

I am not, by any means, unaware of the great and formidable difficulties which lie in the way of the accomplishment of these results. But what are difficulties in the presence of the

Almighty, the Eternal Spirit? If the promise and the oath of God are pledged for their accomplishment, what else does our faith need to rest upon? Our glorified Christ has provided for the full and complete redemption of our humanity and our world, and "he will not fail nor be discouraged" until this work is done. In harmony with this provision, ay, as an integral part of this provision, the Comforter has come forth to complete and consummate this work. And this he has been and still is doing gloriously. Invisible to the human eye, he is acting directly upon human souls, bowing them down by his power, illuminating them with his light, lifting them up from their degradation and ruin, transforming them by his grace, restraining often, even where he does not renew, and checking where he does not convert; ceaselessly active by day and by night, in all countries and in all climes, never losing sight for one moment of his great purpose, and never relaxing his omnipotent energies. And now, even now, he is ready to come down upon the whole Church and the whole world, and to bring the millions of the world down into the dust at the feet of Jesus.

One thing we must remember here—that all the while he is doing this work he does not testify of himself. Thus the Saviour declared, "He shall not speak of himself; but what he shall hear, that shall he speak." He testifies of Christ. He is drawing the attention of the world to Christ. And there never was the time when all classes of men were so busily engaged in looking at him. Men cannot keep their eyes off him. He is hated and despised by multitudes; his divinity and authority are denied, and yet they keep looking at him and his cross. Strauss and Renan, Parker and Emerson, and a host of other names, have called the attention of millions to his claims, who otherwise might not have thought of them. Their utterances are listened to by the world, but when they have died away the name of Jesus is plowed deeper into the hearts of men than ever before. Just as, during the prevalence of the storm, the sun is obscured by heavy masses of clouds, but when the storm is over we forget the blackened sky, the clouds, and the tempest, and see only the sun enthroned in the heavens and flooding the world with his glory; so men rage against Christ, and sometimes, for a season, may obscure his glory by their sophistries or their wrath; but the storm passes over, the clouds are brushed away, and we see Jesus sitting upon the throne of the universe, and on "his head are many crowns." Or, as on the Mount of Transfiguration, when the cloud came down upon its brow, the disciples feared as they entered into it, and there was a voice sounding out from the excellent glory, and Moses and Elijah were manifested; but when the cloud was lifted up "*they saw no man, save Jesus only.*" So the Comforter will exalt Jesus before the world, and even the whole universe. For "unto him every knee shall bow, and every tongue confess that he is Lord, to the glory of God the Father." He is now convincing the world more fully than at any previous time that its great sin is unbelief in Christ; that the source of its righteousness is only to be found in Christ, and that Christ is to be the final judge of all its inhabitants. And not only so; he is taking of the things of Christ and showing them to his people as never before. He is uncovering the depths of their corruptions in order to lead them to the fountain of his blood, where all may be washed away. He is opening up their eyes to see the length and breadth and height of Christ's redeeming love. Under his inspiring presence and power they are awakening to gird themselves with his own divine strength, and to robe themselves in the beautiful, spotless garments of the Redeemer's righteousness. And when they shall be thus girded and thus robed, they will radiate the world with his reflected glory, and shake it to its very center by his imparted power. One only condition is essential in order to realize this wonderful gift of the Comforter for the production of these grand results, and that is, *believing prayer.* O ye servants and handmaids of the Lord, "keep not silence, and give the Lord no rest until he establish, and until he make Jerusalem a praise in the earth!" God is now moving wonderfully among the nations. Thrones of tyranny and oppression are crumbling into the dust; hoary systems of error and superstition are passing away; a mighty upheaval is now going on; all men are looking on, and wondering what will come next. O blessed, Holy Comforter, finish speedily thy great work in this world! Amen, and Amen!

VENI CREATOR SPIRITUS.

I.

Veni, Creator Spiritus,
Mentes tuorum visita,
Imple superna gratia,
Quæ tu creasti pectora.

II.

Qui Paraclitus diceris
Donum Dei altissimi,
Fons vivus, ignis, charitas,
Et spiritalis unctio.

III.

Tu septiformis munere,
Dextræ Dei tu digitus,
Tu rite promissum Patris,
Sermone ditans guttura.

IV.

Accende lumen sensibus,
Infunde amorem cordibus,
Infirma nostri corporis,
Virtute firmans perpeti.

VENI CREATOR SPIRITUS.

TRANSLATED BY ABRAHAM COLES, M. D., PH. D.

I.

Creator, Spirit, Guest Divine,
Come, visit and inhabit Thine ;
Enter the mind's most holy place,
And breasts Thou madest fill with grace.

II.

Thou who art called the Paraclete,
Of God Most High the Gift Complete,
The living Fount, the Fire, the Love,
And Holy Unction from above.

III.

Sevenfold the gifts at Thy command,
Finger of God's supreme right hand,
The promise of the Father, who
Dost throats enrich with utt'rance new.

IV.

Kindle the senses, light impart ;
Infuse Thy love in every heart ;
Weaken our body's bent to wrong ;
In lasting virtue making strong.

V.

Hoftem repellas longius,
Pacemque dones protinus ;
Ductore sic te prævio
Vitemus omne noxium.

VI.

Per te sciamus da Patrem
Noscamus atque Filium,
Teque utriusque Spiritum
Credamus omni tempore.

VII.

Deo Patri fit gloria
Et Filio, qui a mortuis
Surrexit, ac Paraclito
In sæculorum sæcula.

CAROLUS MAGNUS.

V.

Drive farther off the hellish foe,
And constant peace henceforth bestow.
May we—Thou, Leader in the way—
All evil shun, nor go astray.

VI.

Grant we may know in verity
The Father and the Son through Thee;
And in all time may Thee believe
Spirit of Both, and so receive.

VII.

Be God the Father glorified,
And God the Son who for us died
And rose, and God the Paraclete,
Ages on ages infinite.

CHARLEMAGNE, (beginning of ninth century.)

THE END.

www.ingramcontent.com/pod-product-compliance
Lightning Source LLC
LaVergne TN
LVHW020244110826
845151LV00003B/1021